This book was designed by
Olo Éditions
36, rue Laffitte
75009 Paris
France
www.oloeditions.com

original concept marçais and marchand
editor nicolas marçais
art director philippe marchand
authors serge bueno and gilles lhote
translator roland glasser
layout thomas hamel
image editing s2synergy global

First published in the United States of America in 2020 by
Universe Publishing, A Division of
Rizzoli International Publications, Inc.
300 Park Avenue South
New York, NY 10010
www.rizzoliusa.com

Originally published in French in 2020 by
éditions Gründ

© 2020 Olo Éditions

Printed in South Korea

2020 2021 2022 2023 / 10 9 8 7 6 5 4 3 2 1

ISBN: 978-0-7893-3954-6
Library of Congress Control Number: 2020937083

Visit us online:
Facebook.com/RizzoliNewYork
Twitter: @Rizzoli_Books
Instagram.com/RizzoliBooks
Pinterest.com/RizzoliBooks
Youtube.com/user/RizzoliNY
Issuu.com/Rizzoli

HEROES MOTORS®
LOS ANGELES

SERGE BUENO   GILLES LHOTE

THE ART OF
THE VINTAGE
MOTORCYCLE
1905   1955
BY HEROES MOTORS, LOS ANGELES
The Original

UNIVERSE

When Frenchman Serge Bueno, a specialist in the restoration of top-of-the-line classic motorcycles, opened Heroes Motors in Los Angeles, it was a revolution in the world of traditional motorcycle shops.

Every model sold in his three Los Angeles concept stores (La Brea, Melrose, Malibu)—each an elegant blend of gallery/workshop/boutique with a rock vibe—is an exceptional piece. A graduate of the prestigious Beaux-Arts de Paris, Serge is an artist, an engineer, and a designer. He is a purist who is as demanding as a high-end couturier and is gifted with a surgical precision to rival those who craft the finest luxury watches. Collectors from all over the world, as well as rocker arm aficionados, knowledgeable enthusiasts, lovers of exquisite finishes, and museum directors flock to his deluxe workshop to buy the spectacular creations of this engineering whiz.

Portrait of a Motorcycle Hero

Motorcycles are a serious business in the Bueno family. Serge's father was a motorcycle fanatic and when Serge was ten years old, he too was bitten by the bug upon seeing his brother's Yamaha TY50.

The teenage Serge began dreaming of the United States as he read *Moto Verte*, a magazine that recounted the exploits of the supercross riders who trained out in sunny California—the home of Kustom Kulture and Hollywood, surf culture and general coolness, with a plethora of motorcycle workshops. In short, California symbolized the American Dream of legend, and this dream would stay with him. When he was nineteen, Serge bought his first motorcycle—a Yamaha XT 600—and rode down toward Saint-Tropez in the South of France in search of adventure and the sun he loves so much. The trip gave him a taste for cruising, American style. But since he also had a passion for drawing, painting, and photography, Serge decided to study at the Beaux-Arts de Paris. Some years passed and Serge found himself earning a living in IT, having started his own company. It was demanding work requiring total commitment, but he never gave up on his first love as he spent his weekends in his garage tinkering away on old motorcycles he found here and there, slowly restoring them. He did it all himself: engine, chassis, and paintwork. His first restoration project was a 1936 Peugeot 350, which he discovered in a junk store in the Paris suburb of Vincennes. Serge did not yet realize that he was in the process of learning the craft that would fundamentally change his life.

At the age of forty, this visionary entrepreneur decided to sell his IT company and focus on his main passion: the restoration of exceptional motorcycles. He already had a collection of several dozen cult pieces—including a 1920 Indian Daytona, an Indian PowerPlus, and a very rare Harley-Davidson ID model—and had earned himself a solid reputation. With nothing left to prove in France, Serge wanted to explore the American market. He carefully packed his treasures into crates and put them in storage—they would join him in Los Angeles at a later date—and took a plane to California, which had always fueled his wildest dreams.

Serge no longer wished to remain a spectator. He wanted to play an active role in that legendary movieland forged by such rebel motorcycle heroes as Marlon Brando, Steve McQueen, Peter Fonda, Dennis Hopper, and the stuntman Evel Knievel. This was the America portrayed in *The Wild One* and *Easy Rider*. It was also the place where all those genius mechanics, piston-head sorcerers, and Gyro Gearloose types were constantly reinventing the classic motorcycle movement.

Go West!

The maiden voyage of this perfectionist would last six long months, at the end of which Serge decided to remain in California and try his luck in the City of Angels. His wife, Muriel, and his children joined him for this new start and a future that, as uncertain as it might have been, was so promising. Together they would write the pages of a new life. Serge wanted to instill in his children the idea that nothing is impossible and to teach them the importance of hard work, perseverance, and passion.

Serge realized that it was here in California that the most important auctions took place—those drawing the wealthiest collectors—that the market for the restoration of high-end prestige motorcycles remained wide open, and that the climate was really beneficial; the low humidity level lowered risks of corrosion.

Ever the cunning businessman, Serge fell in love with District La Brea. Here, among art galleries, hip fashion outlets, and hipster restaurants, he took a lease on an old, abandoned warehouse that had gone unnoticed. He found it thanks to Thierry Guetta—better known as the street artist Mr. Brainwash—whose own incredible adventure had started in that very spot: "This place brought me luck. It's protected by a star. It will do the same for you!"

Serge spent three months renovating the derelict premises and transforming the space according to his vision. With his own hands, he built it out to showcase the most beautiful classic motorcycles. Mr. Brainwash was right: on the day after opening, Serge sold his first motorcycle, a Vincent—the Bentley of bikes—a marvel that was worth a fortune. The sale allowed this Frenchman to join the Southern California Vincent Owners Club, with access to its very elite address book.

Heroes Motors: A Concept Is Born

It was a massive job to re-create the world of an old-style motorcycle shop tinged with a 1950s rock 'n' roll vibe, mixed with that antiquated yet friendly atmosphere so characteristic of spaces that are charged with history: black leather sofas, studiously rusted shelves, glossy illustrated books placed on classy coffee tables, and impeccably framed sepia photographs. In short, a rough-edged chic spot where customers could relax with a drink while admiring the fine collection of treasures.

Of course the 1918 Indian Factory Racer, the 1920 Harley-Davidson, and the 1933 Chicago Factory Racer take pride of place, but Serge's strength lies in also restoring, displaying, and selling foreign motorcycles. There the main criteria are quality, reputation, and rarity. Among a 1903 Peugeot Factory Racer, a 1930 Matchless G45, a 1971 BSA Scrambler B25 Sport, you might find an extremely rare 1920 Excelsior Series 20 Big Twin, a fantastic 1920 Gillet Factory Racer, or a 1930 Monet-Goyon competing for space with a 1926 Magnat-Debon Racer, not to mention the supremely sublime red 1929 Majestic—a forgotten treasure commissioned and purchased by the big-time collector Bobby Haas, the owner of the Haas Moto Museum in Dallas.

Heroes Motors: A Shooting Star

Collectors from all over the world rushed to make their pilgrimage to the new holy of holies of motorcycles in La Brea. Movie stars soon followed—the ultimate proof of success in Hollywood. At Heroes Motors, you might run into Arnold Schwarzenegger (the Terminator himself), Keanu Reeves (*The Matrix*, *John Wick*), Olivier Martinez, Liev Schreiber (who plays the title character in the series *Ray Donovan*), the producer Peter M. Lenkov, the Stallone brothers, and Cody Walker (brother of the late Paul Walker of the *Fast and Furious* franchise), as well as the cream of California rock music.

Melrose: in the wake of such success and renown, Serge opened his second shop on another trendy avenue in Los Angeles. The atmosphere is the same: leather, wood, glass, a rusty patina that is just right, and workshops that are as pristine as operating rooms, where new life is breathed into these mechanized legends of the past that were so revolutionary in their time.

Serge's motto remains unchanged: "Bring back to life exceptional motorcycles for eternity, historic models such as the Flying Merkel or the Cyclone." And the recipe for his growing success stays the same: eighteen-hour working days, endless scouring of motorcycle shows all over the world, and the hunt for small collectors out in the backcountry or the desert— purists who agree to sell their treasures, for they know that Serge Bueno will restore the machines' former luster and make them roar again. Recently, at the request of the owner of Malibu Country Mart—a high-end boutique mall that has only luxury brands—Serge finished building out his third Heroes Motors, still with his own hands. Located just a few yards from the Pacific Coast Highway, which has seen some of the most iconic motorcycles rumble down its asphalt, these new premises have retained the classic Heroes Motors chic with an added touch of Malibu surfer vibe. Cherry on the gas tank: Serge is in discussion with Keanu Reeves to sell the star's own motorcycles at Heroes Motors.

We worked for many months with Serge to produce this book, in which each machine—a relic of its time—is presented as a sublime work of art. Every one of these motorcycles belonged to and was restored with love and passion by the artist himself. Even more incredibly, all of the photographs were also shot by Serge, who turned his garage into a studio, endeavoring to find the best light and the most flattering angles. Each model, restored or not, becomes an artwork that you could hang on your living room wall, like a painting signed by an old master. We attain perfection here, with the nickel-plating of parts, the very finest bodywork, the gleaming spokes, and the extreme luminosity of the paintwork.

Not content with resuscitating and embellishing these trophies of the past, Serge Bueno also creates life-size bronze sculptures. You will need a very keen eye to tell the difference between the original model and the sculpture.

HEROES MOTORS
WEST HOLLYWOOD
8611 Melrose Avenue
West Hollywood, CA 90069
Phone: 424-382-1049

HEROES MOTORS
MALIBU
Malibu Country Mart "C9"
3835 Cross Creek Road
Malibu, CA 90265
Phone: 424-644-0393

HEROES MOTORS

PEUGEOT
FACTORY RACER · 1905 >010

INDIAN
SINGLE 500 · 1912 >014

FLYING MERKEL
BOARD TRACK RACER · 1912 >024

HARLEY-DAVIDSON
BOARD TRACK RACER
SURVIVOR · 1915 >030

INDIAN
DAYTONA RACER · 1920 >060

MAGNAT-DEBON
RACING 350 · 1921 >066

EXCELSIOR
HENDERSON DELUXE · 1922 >072

HARLEY-DAVIDSON
WF SPORT · 1922 >078

PEUGEOT
P104 · 1926 >106

MONET-GOYON
MC SPORT DELUXE · 1926 >110

BMW
R47 · 1927 >114

TERROT
500 NS SPORT · 1927 >120

NSU
MODEL T SPORT RALLYE · 1929 >152

TERROT
HST 350 SIDE-VALVE · 1929 >158

FN
M67 RACER · 1930 >164

MONET-GOYON
SUPERSPORT · 1930 >170

NORTON
M 30 · 1937 >198

BROUGH SUPERIOR
SS80 · 1938 >202

NORTON
M18 · 1938 >208

BMW
R25 · 1950 >212

PEUGEOT

IN 1898, YEARS BEFORE HARLEY-DAVIDSON AND INDIAN, PEUGEOT BUILT ITS FIRST MOTORCYCLE. THE BRAND WOULD SOON COME TO DOMINATE THE RACING WORLD THROUGH ITS REVOLUTIONARY TECHNICAL INNOVATIONS. IN 1907, THE BRITISH MOTORCYCLE RACER HARRY REMBRANDT "REM" FOWLER WON THE TWIN-CYLINDER CLASS OF THE VERY FIRST ISLE OF MAN TOURIST TROPHY, RIDING A NORTON EQUIPPED WITH A PEUGEOT ENGINE. THREE YEARS EARLIER, IN 1904, THE PEUGEOT CATALOGUE HAD ALREADY FEATURED THREE NEW MODELS, INCLUDING THE SUPERB AND HIGHLY RARE FACTORY RACER.

This close-up—which looks like a hyperrealist painting, with the light perfectly catching the leather, the rubber, and the copper— brings out the nobility and the beauty of this Factory Racer. The patinated leather pouch containing the battery and the greaser matching the color of the gas tank remain the classiest of signatures. The lion brand was indeed the first to produce exceptional motorcycles.

The D-Type was a sleek beast built for speed, propelled by an engine with a displacement of either 300 cc (18.3 cu in) or 330 cc (20.15 cu in)— the model shown here. It offered both power and reliability and was immediately recognizable, thanks to the famous leather pannier mounted in front of the handlebars. This pannier did not contain mail, however, but a large battery to power the spark plug; magneto ignition systems were not yet in common use at the time. The entire motorcycle was conceived and designed with an eye to efficiency and class; one example is the elegant greaser attached to the front fork, which served to oil the hub.

The two little tanks containing oil and the battery compartment, located at the rear of the long gas tank, only added to the superstyled profile. Best of all, this thing of beauty could be ordered with a range of options, such as a bouncy Truffault fork instead of the rigid one, or a chain-drive trans- mission. Only three were ever made, of which just two survive, including this masterpiece brought back to life by Serge Bueno.

This cult motorcycle was ridden by the champion racer Lucien Desvaux in April 1905. It has won numerous awards as well as two prestigious concours d'elégance in California (Beverly Hills and Pebble Beach) and the one at Montlhéry, in France, its country of origin.

It is worth noting that, several months later, Peugeot became the first manufacturer in the world to equip some of its motorcycles with a DOHC (Dual Overhead Camshaft) engine. The first camshaft operates the intake valves, while the second operates the exhaust valves, making the engine more efficient and increasing its performance.

Not only were the Peugeot engineers motorcycle pioneers, they also had a truly admirable workmanship, demonstrating a precision and skill that were revolutionary. This rare Factory Racer is a priceless example of classic mechanical art.

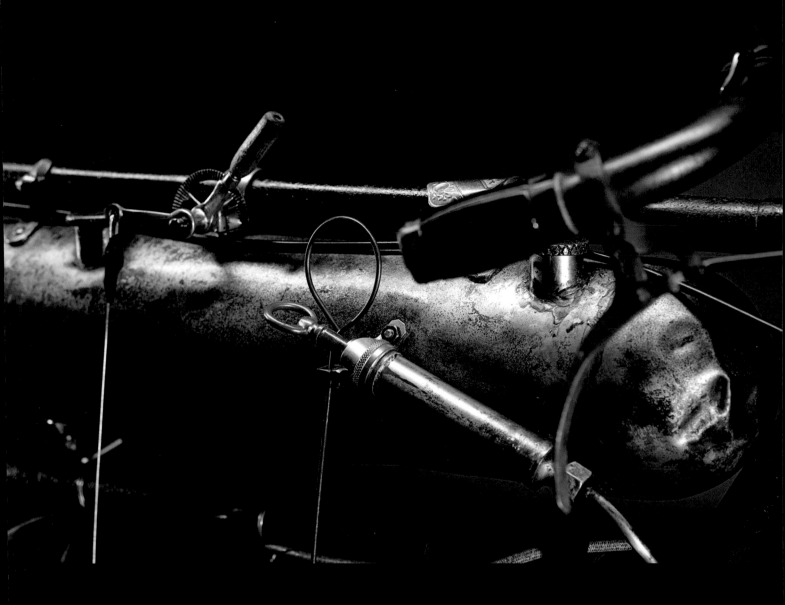

Manufacturer: Peugeot
Year of production: 1905

ENGINE

Type: single-cylinder, four-stroke, air-cooled
Displacement: 330 cc (20.15 cu in)
Power: approx. 5 hp
Gearbox: none
Lubrication: manual via a pump fixed to the side of the gas tank
Transmission: belt, with the option of chain or shaft-and-pinion
Maximum speed: 50 mph

BIKE

Frame: steel, tubular, with engine mounted in the center
Suspension: rigid fork, with the option of a bouncy Truffault fork
Brakes: rear block-brake
Weight: approx. 110 lbs

SINGLE 500cc · 1912 ·
Indian
MOTORCYCLE

THIS INDIAN IS FAMOUS FOR SEVERAL REASONS. FIRST, IT WAS ONE OF THE MANY COLLECTOR'S MOTORCYCLES THAT BELONGED TO STEVE McQUEEN AND WAS SOLD FOR A VERY HIGH PRICE AT AN AUCTION IN LAS VEGAS. SECOND, IT WAS THE FIRST INDIAN MODEL MANUFACTURED WITH A BELT-DRIVE TRANSMISSION, HENCE ITS NICKNAME "BELT DRIVE SINGLE."

The arrival of the Indian Single 500 in 1912 clearly announced a strategy shift toward the future Big Twins, always with great attention to detail.

Right: A period photograph from when Indian was already promoting itself as the brand of elegance, fun, and "riding together."

Up until 1912, all Indians were fitted with chain-drive transmissions, unlike Harley-Davidson, which had long favored belt drives. The Indian engineers were reluctant about belt drives because they had a tendency to slip in wet conditions. So they worked on a new generation of belts that would make them more financially competitive.

The belt drive was not the only innovation on this motorcycle equipped with a 500 cc (30.5 cu in) single-cylinder engine. It also featured air cooling, four-stroke internal combustion, and magneto ignition. These were major improvements, as became clear when the top three places in the 1911 Isle of Man Tourist Trophy were all taken by Indian riders. Their racing machines were then put into full production so that all motorcyclists could enjoy the Belt Drive Single.

In addition to the performance improvements, there were a number of other small ameliorations that allowed this beauty to make up some of its previous lag on Harley-Davidson: a long clutch lever, a band brake (on the rear wheel), a leather saddle with spring suspension, and the not insignificant option of a paintwork in royal blue instead of the scarlet red of the factory model.

This particular 1912 Indian, as well as the 1916 Indian 1000 cc PowerPlus featured later, were both part of the consignment of treasures that were carefully packed up in crates for shipment from France to California when the Bueno family moved to Los Angeles. Serge Bueno bought these two motorcycle heroes in Europe: one from a private seller and the other at an auction.

Manufacturer: Indian
Year of production: 1912

ENGINE

Type: single-cylinder, four-stroke, air-cooled
Displacement: 500 cc (30.5 cu in)
Power: 8 hp
Ignition: Bosch magneto
Gearbox: three-speed, manual shifter
Transmission: belt
Maximum speed: 45 mph

BIKE

Frame: steel, single cradle
Suspension: leaf spring front fork, rigid rear
Brakes: no front brake, rear band brake
Weight: 210 lbs

BOARD TRACK RACERS

•

THE RIGHT STUFF

One of the most popular motorsports in the United States between 1910 and 1930 was motorcycle racing on tracks made of wooden boards. The craze reached its peak during the Roaring Twenties. The top riders of the most famous manufacturers, such as Harley-Davidson, Indian, Henderson, and Excelsior, competed to shatter records. The extreme banking of the tracks increased speeds tremendously and the generous width encouraged spectacular overtaking. The huge stands were filled with excited crowds who lapped up the exploits of these speed heroes astride their mechanized monsters, each outperforming the last.

In 1919, at a speedway in Kansas City, Missouri, Harley-Davidson rider Ralph Hepburn ("Speedy Ralph") was one of the first to cover 100 miles at 85 mph. That same year, Harley introduced a model featuring an innovative horizontally opposed twin-cylinder engine. A little later, Harley's speed team—composed of Hepburn, Fred Ludlow, Leslie "Red" Parkhurst, and Otto Walker—broke the 150 km/h (93 mph) barrier on the raised ring at Rockingham, New Hampshire. The rivalry between Harley-Davidson and the other manufacturers and champions was merciless. Wells Bennett, one of the best long-distance racers and a devotee of the Henderson Four model, had no hesitation in telling journalists that the Henderson Four was the best motorcycle ever built in the United States.

But Harley-Davidson's main competitor was Indian, which boasted riders such as Jim Davis, who smashed many a record on the Altoona Bowl track. Then there was the Los Angeles superstar Johnny Krieger. He crashed halfway through a race at the Rockingham board track as he was negotiating a corner at over 85 mph. He slid for several yards, got up, sorted his bike out, then nonchalantly returned to his hotel as if nothing had happened. This kind of attitude would come to be known as "having the right stuff."

This was a fabulous period during which the major motorcycle brands were constantly improving their machines and taking big mechanical leaps forward, which resulted in the building of motorcycles that are now worth fortunes and are highly sought after by the biggest collectors. Hundreds of board tracks—including the famous ones at Daytona Beach, Florida; Beverly Hills, California; and Baltimore, Maryland—were the scenes of races featuring such legendary board trackers as the 1915 and 1920 Harley-Davidson models, the 1919 and 1920 Indian Daytona models, and, of course, the great 1912 Flying Merkel, the 1915 Cyclone, and the 1922 Excelsior.

At Heroes Motors, the Roaring Twenties are roaring still.

"THE EXTREME BANKING OF THE TRACKS INCREASED SPEEDS TREMENDOUSLY AND THE GENEROUS WIDTH ENCOURAGED SPECTACULAR OVERTAKING."

PROUDLY BORN IN MILWAUKEE

1912

Board Track Racer

FLYING MERKEL

· ORIGINAL COMPANY ·

THIS IS AN ICONIC MOTORCYCLE. IN A SPAN OF JUST FOUR YEARS, FROM 1911 TO 1915, THE VISIONARY JOE MERKEL CREATED SEVERAL EXCEPTIONAL MACHINES, SOME OF WHOSE TECHNICAL ADVANCES INFLUENCED HARLEY-DAVIDSON AND INDIAN. THIS ORANGE QUEEN OF THE SPEEDWAYS FORGED A LEGEND THAT HAS LASTED FOR ALMOST 110 YEARS AND NOW COMMANDS UNHEARD-OF SALE PRICES AT AUCTION.

From Milwaukee to Middletown, Ohio, by way of Miami, Joe Merkel—inventor, rider, and engineer—was driven by an intense passion for mechanics to build the wonderful motorcycles that bear his name. In 1908, he founded the Light Manufacturing and Foundry Company, producing machines with the trademark "Merkel Light" displayed on the tank. Two years later, he was one of the genius pioneers of the twin-cylinder engine. His 884 cc (53.9 cu in) V-twin engines provoked admiration.

In 1911, the company was taken over by the Miami Cycle and Manufacturing Company, which changed the trademark to "Flying Merkel" and supplied the capital for the creation of a small but highly effective speed team that would take on the major manufacturers at every racetrack in the country. The masterstroke was to paint the motorcycles in a striking bright orange that would become commonly known as "Merkel orange."

From the following year, the 1912 Flying Merkel Board Tracker began devouring the wooden boards of the speedways at 60 mph. With its unusual, slightly curved tank, designed to provide more space for the large V-twins, this squat, aggressive speedster did not go unnoticed, becoming a firm favorite with aficionados of the scene. The design of the oil feeder, the new fork (predecessor of the telescopic fork), the fast magneto ignition, and the Schebler carburetor made it a fearsome weapon.

On the track, the riders Maldwyn Jones, Charles Balke, and Stanley Kellogg performed wonders. Fred Whittler broke the 110 km/h (68.5 mph) barrier on the Los Angeles board track, and Maldwyn Jones beat Erwin "Cannonball" Baker in a ten-mile race. The astounding Flying Merkel adventure would come to an end in 1915 due to lack of funds, but the devotion accorded this orange speed demon would never fade. "Old soldiers never die!"

Today, this priceless museum piece holds pride of place suspended from the ceiling of the Heroes Motors boutique in Malibu. Serge Bueno has a

Close-up of the top of the gas tank, which is fitted with an oil pump for easy lubrication of the parts.

particular soft spot for this warhorse because the story of its resurrection is unique. "I arrived very early for the opening of a trade show in Germany and, quite by chance, spotted this holy grail, of which there remained only the frame, the engine, and one pedal. I carefully packed up these pieces in a crate, destination Los Angeles. Extensive, dogged research around the world turned up part of a fork, a chain, and so on. In the end it took me three years of relentless work to breathe life back into this antique that symbolizes the genius and sacrifices of its creator, Joe Merkel."

Manufacturer: Flying Merkel
Year of production: 1912

ENGINE

Type: V-twin, four-stroke, air-cooled
Displacement: 1,000 cc (61 cu in)
Power: 17 hp
Gearbox: none
Ignition: magneto
Lubrication: automatic oil-drip feeder, manual pump
Clutch: none
Secondary transmission: double chain
Maximum speed: approx. 75 mph

BIKE

Frame: steel, tubular, loop
Suspension: truss front fork, rigid rear
Brakes: none
Weight: approx. 220 lbs

Anatomy of an unusual speedway beast: the curved gas tank designed to accommodate the height of the V-twins and which also includes an oil pump; the two-speed chain-drive transmission; and this crazy V-twin with twin exhausts.

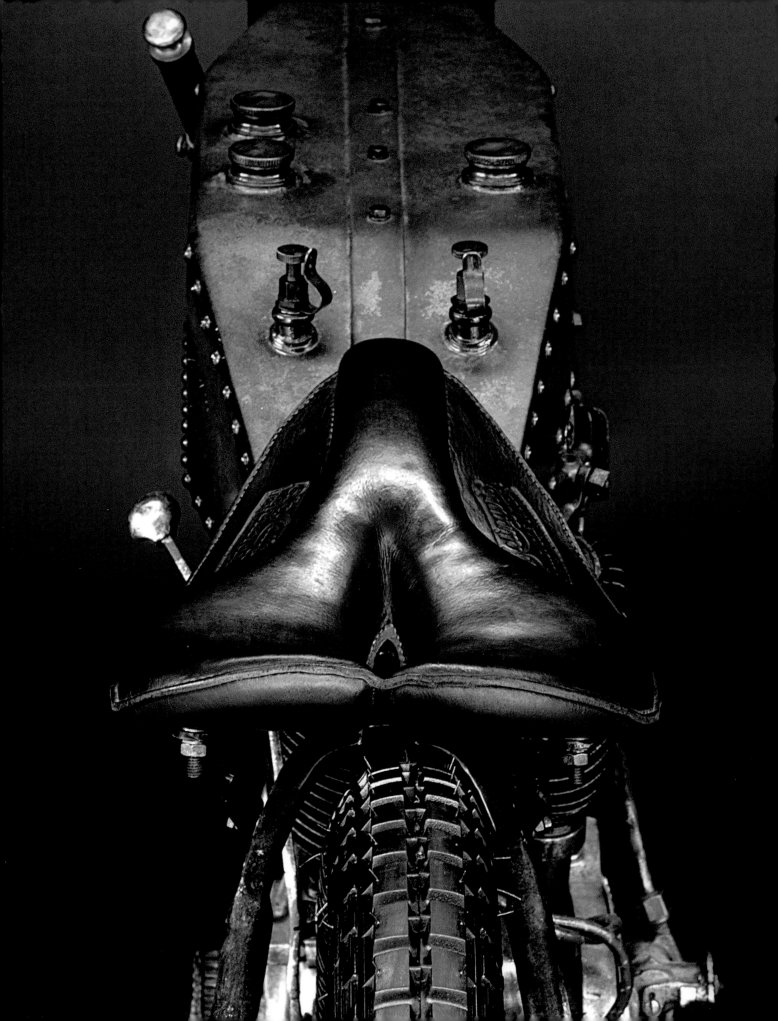

BOARD TRACK RACER SURVIVOR

1915

HARLEY-DAVIDSON

COMPANY

Original

IN 1914, HARLEY-DAVIDSON DECIDED TO JOIN THE RACING GAME AND GET EVEN WITH INDIAN BY COMPETING ON THE BOARD TRACKS. TO DO THIS, THE MILWAUKEE COMPANY HIRED WILLIAM "BILL" OTTAWAY, A BRILLIANT ENGINEER WHO WAS ALSO AN EXCELLENT RIDER AND TACTICIAN. OTTAWAY WORKED FOR MONTHS IN GREAT SECRECY TO PERFECT A MACHINE CAPABLE OF BEATING HARLEY'S RIVALS. IT WAS CALLED THE 11K.

Who would believe that this motorcycle, photographed from this angle and in this light, is 105 years old? It is much lesser known than other Harleys, but still historically important.

t the finish of the 300-mile race at the Dodge City track, in Kansas, on July 14, 1915, the 11K Board Track Racer entered into glory when Harley-Davidson placed six of its team's riders in the top seven places. The winner was Leslie "Red" Parkhurst, a motorcycle hero we will learn more about later. Bill Ottaway had really pushed the envelope to achieve this super Harley, which some people dubbed "The Flying Saucer." The eight-valve V-twin engine (1,000 cc/ 61 cu in) was so tall that they had to create concave sections in the gas tank to accommodate it.

Everything was bespoke: the eight-lobe camshaft, the gear-driven oil pump, the crankcase covers, and the flywheel—a mechanical device designed to store and release rotational energy. Add a three-speed gearbox—to which the kick starter pedal was attached by a sliding gear mechanism—and direct transmission by chain drive, and you have one of the very first custom Harleys. It is true that with its dropped handlebars, visible rivets, and its army-green paint, the 11K looked mean and ready to tear up the track. In 1915, Harley's racing crew—nicknamed "The Eight Valves Team"—won many other competitions. They were more than ready to hurtle into the 1920s.

This motorcycle garnered such enthusiasm that Harley-Davidson put it in its catalogue with a range of different options for wheel size, seat, transmission, and chassis. This was unique for the brand—something never done before. For the first time in company history, the Milwaukee manufacturer put a factory racing model on general sale.

Manufacturer: Harley-Davidson
Year of production: 1915

ENGINE

Type: V-twin, four-stroke, air-cooled, eight-valve
Displacement: 1,000 cc (61 cu in)
Power: approx. 17 hp
Gearbox: none
Transmission: chain (primary and secondary)
Maximum speed: approx. 95 mph

BIKE

Frame: steel, tubular, single cradle
Suspension: springer front fork, rigid rear
Brakes: none
Weight: 220 lbs

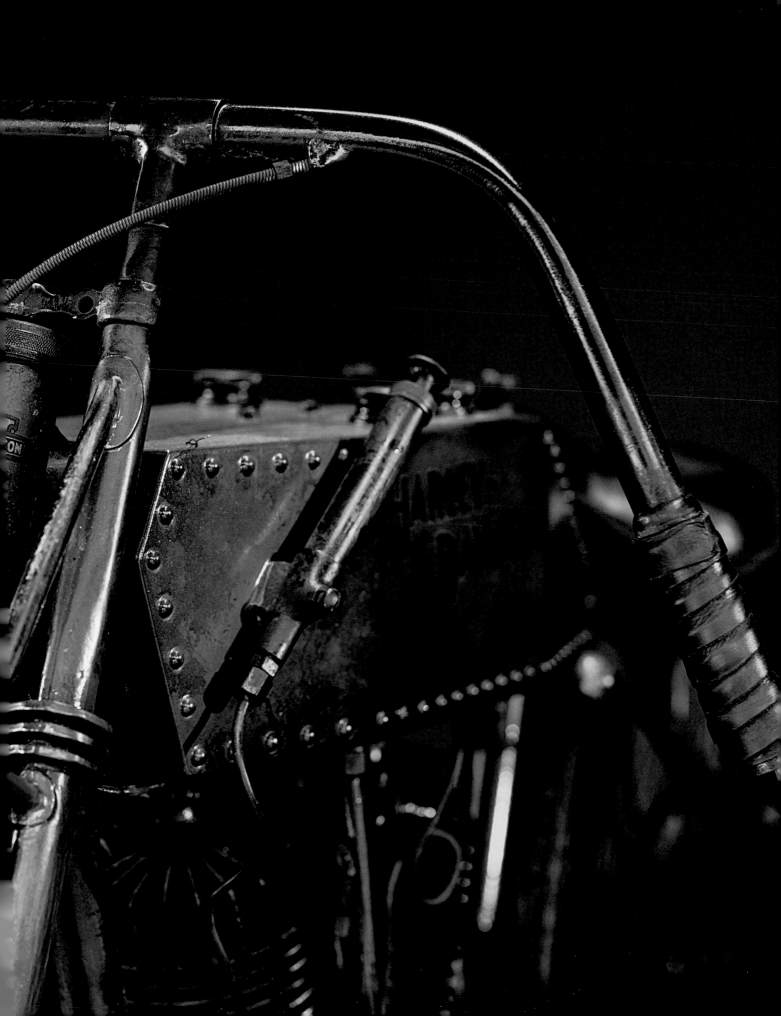

THE RARE AND PRICELESS 1915 CYCLONE BOARD TRACK RACER (FROM THE SUBLIME COLLECTION OF STEVE McQUEEN) WAS THE TALK OF THE TOWN WHEN IT WAS PUT UP FOR AUCTION. IT IS THE UNCONTESTED HISTORIC SUPERSTAR OF ALL MOTORCYCLE AUCTIONS, HAVING SOLD FOR $852,000, AND IS NOW OFTEN REFERRED TO SIMPLY AS THE "STEVE McQUEEN." STORY OF A SOLID GOLD SPEED DEMON.

Like its rival the Flying Merkel, the Cyclone had a very short life span (from 1912 to 1917), which no doubt explains the extraordinary prices the two shooting stars fetch today. The Cyclone was built by the Joerns Motor Manufacturing Company based in St. Paul, Minnesota, before moving to Sheboygan, Wisconsin. Conceived and designed by the engineer Andrew Strand, this yellow arrow is the perfect example of elegant simplicity and extreme efficiency. It is a mechanical beast sleekly encased in yellow.

The Flying Merkel had its blazing orange, the Indian its scarlet red. As for the Cyclone, it was painted in "Joerns canary yellow," a color so flashy that it jumped right out of photographs. Now there's a genius advertising idea! With its powerful V-twin engine (1,000 cc/61 cu in), which was designed specifically for speed, the Cyclone soon started winning on the most popular racetracks. In 1914, a rider on his canary yellow steed even managed to beat an Excelsior in a fast 'n' dirty One Mile speed race, reaching an estimated top speed of 71.5 mph. Sadly, owing to cash flow problems, Joerns decided to disband its speed team in 1917 and close down production.

This dream motorcycle provided a new passion project for Serge Bueno who, by the most fortunate stroke of chance, came across a few parts of this artifact at another auction. "I couldn't believe my eyes; there was just a section of the frame, some engine pieces, and part of the handlebars. I think I have a lucky star looking out for me!" Serge packed this incomplete jigsaw of a Cyclone into a case and shipped it to Los Angeles, where he spent many years sourcing and re-creating new identical parts, in order to restore Steve McQueen's favorite motorcycle to its former magnificence.

Bobby Haas, the owner of the Haas Moto Museum in Dallas, commissioned a life-size bronze sculpture of this classic Cyclone. He would go on to commission three other sculptures: a Flying Merkel, a Henderson, and an Indian. It can be quite hard to distinguish the original from the artwork.

Aesthetic perfection in yellow and black: the period leather helmet adds an extra touch to the phenomenal history of this work of mechanical art.

Three-quarter view of the canary-yellow arrow that shot around the racetracks; and a close-up of the powerful V-twin engine displacing 1,000 cc (61 cu in)—a single overhead camshaft model.

Manufacturer: Cyclone
Years of production: 1912–17

ENGINE

Type: V-twin, four-stroke, single overhead camshaft, air-cooled
Displacement: 1,000 cc (61 cu in)
Power: 17 hp
Gearbox: none
Secondary transmission: chain
Maximum speed: 110 mph

BIKE

Frame: steel, tubular, loop
Suspension: Druid type front fork with no shock absorption, rigid rear
Brakes: none
Weight: 220 lbs

The characteristic rounded headlight and horn of the PowerPlus, and the famous Indian logo painted on the gas tank.

THIS WONDER OF AESTHETICS AND CONSIDERABLE MECHANICAL PROGRESS WAS THE WORK OF CHARLES GUSTAFSON, THE GENIUS ENGINEER OF THE HENDEE MANUFACTURING COMPANY BASED IN SPRINGFIELD, MASSACHUSETTS. PRODUCED FROM 1916 TO 1923, THE INDIAN 1000 CC POWERPLUS IS A HIGH-PERFORMANCE MONSTER THAT USHERED IN THE ERA OF VERY HIGH ENGINE DISPLACEMENTS AND FIERCE COMPETITION AMONG THE MANUFACTURERS IN THIS CATEGORY.

Above: Indian, which was Harley-Davidson's main competitor for many years, very quickly churned out advertising campaigns, both in the press and in catalogues, where its motorcycles conveyed a promise of adventure and the open road.

At the start of the movie *Duck, You Sucker!*, the cool character John Mallory, an explosives expert, played by James Coburn, arrives in Mexico riding a magnificent Indian PowerPlus—proof of the massive impact that this classic machine had on the collective unconscious. This twin-cylinder, side-valve V engine was the first ever flathead in the company's history.

There were many other innovations, such as the two twist grips at the ends of the very long handlebars. The left-hand one controlled the throttle, while the right-hand one advanced or retarded the spark. For greater ease of use, the three main controls were placed on the right side of the gas tank. They comprised three long vertical levers that operated the exhaust valve lifter, the gear shifter, and the clutch pedal (located on the left-hand side of the motorcycle). As for the suspension, the front had a trailing link fork with leaf spring, while the rear was either rigid (standard) or with a swingarm linked by struts to leaf springs. The PowerPlus had no front brakes, but a rear internal drum brake with an exterior band brake. A three-speed gearbox, a 2.5 gal (9.5 L) gas tank, and long, enveloping mudguards completed the up-to-date fittings of this bright-red rocket topped with a leather spring-mounted saddle.

This motorcycle, which caused a sensation for many years, maintains all of its sleekness and sense of refined power when photographed from any angle. It took Serge Bueno many hours of work and sourcing of parts to revive this star motorcycle that saw the light of day in 1916 and the dawn of the Roaring Twenties, that golden age of two-wheeled speedsters.

Manufacturer: Indian

Years of production: 1916–23

ENGINE

Type: V-twin, four-stroke, air-cooled, side-valve

Displacement: 1,000 cc (61 cu in)

Power: 16 hp

Clutch: pedal

Gearbox: separated three-speed, manual shifter

Transmission: chain (primary and secondary)

Maximum speed: 60 mph

BIKE

Frame: steel, single cradle

Suspension: trailing link front fork with leaf spring, rigid rear with the option of a swingarm linked by struts to leaf springs

Brakes: no front brake, rear internal drum brake with an exterior band brake

Weight: 310 lbs

UPON ITS RELEASE, THE 1918 INDIAN BOARD TRACK RACER WAS CALLED "AN ORIGINAL AMERICAN SUPERBIKE" BECAUSE IT WAS THE JEWEL IN A LINE OF MOTORCYCLES (PRODUCED UNTIL 1923) THAT CHARLES GUSTAFSON, CHIEF ENGINEER OF THE HENDEE MANUFACTURING COMPANY, DUBBED THE "POWERPLUS." WE PRESENT TO YOU THIS QUEEN OF THE SPEEDWAYS IN BOTH ITS ORIGINAL STATE WHEN SERGE BUENO FOUND IT, AS WELL AS IN ITS "MUSEUM" STATE FOLLOWING RESTORATION IN THE HEROES MOTORS WORKSHOP.

The state of preservation of this original Board Track Racer from 1918 was astonishing, as is its exceptional restoration.

Equipped with a 1,000 cc (61 cu in) V-twin engine, this motorcycle signaled the transition from a certain amateurism in speed racing (no helmet, no brake, no suspension) to the professionalism of the 1920s—the golden age of the board tracks when all of the mechanical innovations developed for racing were rolled out into mass production. It is also worth remembering that the United States had just come out of World War I, during which Harley-Davidson and Indian had contributed massively to the war effort by building military motorcycles and sidecars.

When Serge Bueno bought this 1918 Indian racer from a collector who owned many other sought-after motorcycles, he was surprised at its state of preservation, since the motorcycle was, for once, 85 percent complete. He simply had to reconstruct the gas tank, change two pistons and the fork, and redo the saddlery. In addition, he took everything to pieces to remove rust, checked and retuned the engine, nickel-plated parts, rebuilt the wheels and the spokes, then reassembled them all into this beauty: the symbol and the perfect prototype of the incredible popularity surrounding board track racing.

Manufacturer: Indian
Years of production: 1918–23

ENGINE

Type: V-twin, four-stroke, air-cooled
Displacement: 1,000 cc (61 cu in)
Power: 17 hp
Gearbox: none
Secondary transmission: chain
Maximum speed: 100 mph

BIKE

Frame: steel, tubular, loop
Suspension: suspension-less front fork, rigid rear
Brakes: none
Weight: approx. 220 lbs

BOARD TRACK RACER
1920

HARLEY-DAVIDSON
COMPANY

Original

THE NEW DECADE HAD ARRIVED. WITH IT CAME A LOAD OF MECHANICAL ADVANCEMENTS THAT WERE TESTED TO THE EXTREME ON THE BOARD TRACKS BY THE VARIOUS MOTORCYCLE MANUFACTURERS. HARLEY-DAVIDSON STAMPED ITS MARK ON THE EPOCH WITH A RAMPAGING BEAST: THE BOARD TRACK RACER.

"I stored certain motorcycles, such as this Harley, in packing cases like fine wine. And when I opened them in Los Angeles, I realized that my passion and my instinct had not deceived me."

Serge Bueno

fter a short pause in competition, due to the intensive manufacture of military motorcycles that were sent to Europe during World War I, the Milwaukee firm once more asked its tame magician Bill Ottaway to draw up a fresh strategy and reorganize his speed team. Magic Bill hired Leslie "Red" Parkhurst and Otto Walker, two motorcycle heroes whose names would soon be on everyone's lips.

Keen strategist that he was, Ottaway also revolutionized the deployment of personnel at the racetrack, having sensed that it was during pit stops that precious seconds could be gained. Henceforth, wheels were changed in ten to fifteen seconds, oil and gas fill-ups happened faster thanks to wider spouts, and riders wore goggles that would be cleaned each time they stopped.

Finally, in 1920, Ottaway revealed his secret weapon: the new Board Track Racer with its 1,000 cc (61 cu in) twin-cam, eight-valve V-twin engine equipped with a brand-new lubrication system. That year, Jim Davis won the Dodge City race and Ray Weishaar won the 200-miler in Marion, Indiana. And Parkhurst, who had been riding for Harley since 1914, smashed an impressive number of records. In February, he won a slew of speed races over short distances at Daytona Beach, Florida. In June, at Sheepshead Bay, in Brooklyn—considered the fastest speed track in the world at the time—he shattered the world distance record by clocking up 1,452.75 miles in twenty-four hours in driving rain. The following year, this speed champ quit Harley-Davidson to join the rival Excelsior.

Although this marvelous 1920 Harley-Davidson Board Track Racer—ideally designed for speed—has a lower public profile than other motorcycles, it is an astonishing example of mechanized power and racing class. The machine already bears those hallmarks of a classic Harley that have sustained the Wisconsin brand's celebrated status until today. Serge Bueno spent many weeks shuttered in his lair on La Brea Avenue, patiently and lovingly restoring this speedster—bought in a pitiful state—that symbolizes the Americana he adores so much.

Manufacturer: Harley-Davidson
Year of production: 1920

Type: V-twin, four-stroke, air-cooled, eight-valve, pressurized lubrication
Displacement: 1,000 cc (61 cu in)
Power: 18 hp
Ignition: magneto
Gearbox: none
Transmission: chain (primary and secondary)
Maximum speed: 120 mph

Frame: steel, tubular, single cradle
Suspension: springer front fork, rigid rear
Brakes: none
Weight: approx. 200 lbs

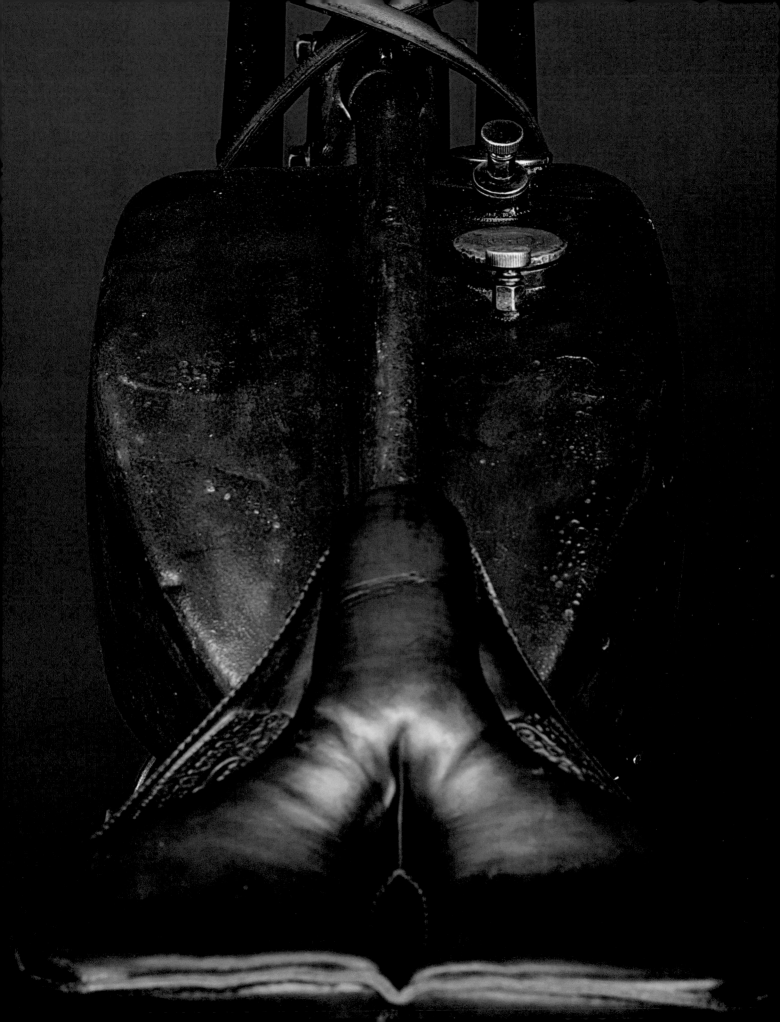

STEVE McQUEEN CLEARLY LOVED INDIAN MOTORCYCLES, AND THIS 1920 DAYTONA MODEL COMES FROM HIS SUPERB COLLECTION. THE MAN WHO DID THE ROUNDS OF THE COLLECTORS, SEEKING OUT THE FINEST MOTORCYCLES ON BEHALF OF THE SUPERSTAR, WAS A TALENTED FELLOW BY THE NAME OF STEPHEN WRIGHT. HE PURCHASED THIS HISTORIC RACER FROM HERBERT WEBB, A COLLECTOR AND INDIAN DEALER IN ROANOKE, VIRGINIA, AND RESTORED IT FOR McQUEEN.

View of the new, lower saddle, whose position slightly changed the look of the gas tank built into the frame.

This Daytona did not reach the dizzying price of the 1912 Indian Single 500 CC when it was sold at auction by Bonhams, but it still sold for $150,000. According to legend, the factory prototype of the Daytona was tested for months by Erwin "Cannonball" Baker, the top dog of Indian riders.

Steve McQueen had specific reasons for acquiring this queen of speed. The motorcycle had several particularities, starting with its Harley-style frame—open at the bottom—that used the engine as a stressed member, and an "S" shaped seat tube. The *Bullitt* actor was also attracted by the innovative 1,000 cc (61 cu in) flathead side-valve V-twin engine developed by Charles Gustafson, which provided superior power, hence its name: "PowerPlus." Also note the lower seat position that gave the rider a more aerodynamic posture and involved slightly modifying the shape of the gas tank by flattening it. The transmission included a clutch, a starter, and a three-speed gearbox.

It is said that riders used to refer to this machine as the "Survivor" because when riding flat out, barely using the rear brake, you had to be a survivor to finish in one piece.

Manufacturer: Indian
Year of production: 1920

ENGINE

Type: V-twin, four-stroke, air-cooled, side-valves
Displacement: 1,000 cc (61 cu in)
Power: approx. 23 hp
Transmission: chain (primary and secondary)
Gearbox: none
Maximum speed: approx. 100 mph

BIKE

Frame: steel, single "keystone" cradle (uses the engine as a stressed member)
Suspension: leaf-spring front fork, rigid rear
Brakes: none
Weight: approx. 220 lbs

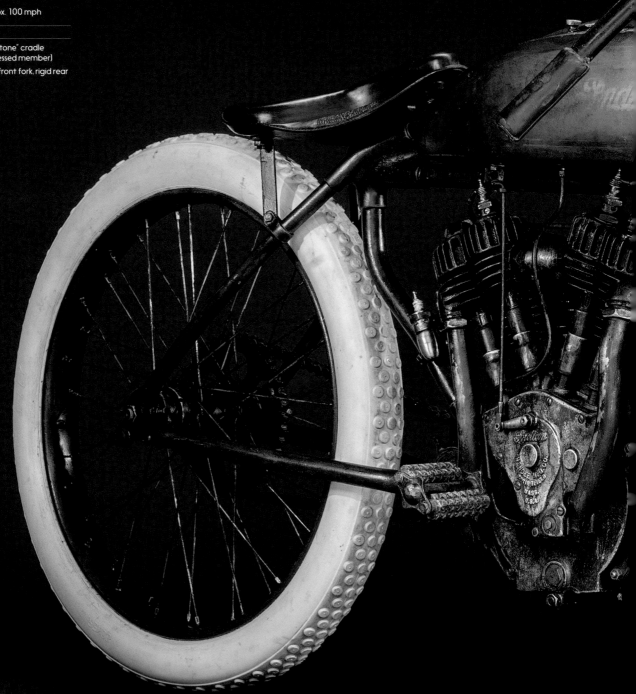

Two Indian Daytonas restored by Heroes Motors. With the one on the left, the approach was very much to preserve its original, vintage state, whereas with the one on the right, the aim was to create a museum piece—a work of art that attracts the biggest collectors.

FOUNDED BY JOSEPH MAGNAT AND LOUIS DEBON
IN LYON, FRANCE, IN 1893, THIS RENOWNED
MANUFACTURER ORIGINALLY SPECIALIZED
IN HIGH-QUALITY BICYCLES. IN 1902, THE
TWO PARTNERS DECIDED TO VENTURE INTO THE
FALTERING MOTORCYCLE MARKET BY CREATING
THE *AUTOCYCLETTE*, A HYBRID MACHINE THAT MIGHT
BEST BE DESCRIBED AS A BICYCLE FITTED WITH
A DE DION-BOUTON ENGINE. IN 1905, HAVING MOVED
THEIR BASE TO GRENOBLE, THESE PIONEERS
PRODUCED THEIR FIRST COMMERCIAL MOTORCYCLE.
IN 1921, THE COMPANY MERGED WITH TERROT—
THE GIANT RIVAL MANUFACTURER BASED IN DIJON.

"The Star of the Alps."
This metal badge attached
to the top tube depicts
the Magnat-Debon logo
(a globe) surmounted by a
star, symbolizing the brand's
ambition and vision. Indeed,
one of this manufacturer's
slogans was "the brand
of connoisseurs."

hen the two visionaries, Magnat and Debon, began developing motorcycles, they had the excellent idea of hiring the engineer and rider Joseph Delamanche and appointing him head of development and motorized two-wheeled vehicles. The result was the Magnat-Debon Racing, which left the workshop in 1921. This exceptional French machine surprised everyone when it hit the racetracks and began winning. It was equipped with a single-cylinder, four-stroke 350 cc (21.35 cu in) "sport cycle" engine with large diameter side valves, and had a myriad of other technological innovations: semiautomatic carburetor with two levers, aluminum pistons, spring-loaded telescopic front fork, high-tension magneto ignition with variable advance, and three-speed gearbox with hand shifter. This speedster could reach 60 mph.

Serge Bueno found this little beauty as a wreck at an auction house near Lyon. "It was carnage; everything was damaged, bent, broken, rusted, and ripped apart. There were loads of parts missing. The entire restoration took more than three weeks. I rebuilt it all, from the kick starter to the clutch—friction plate with cork inserts—by way of the engine lubrication system—manual oil pump—the sport exhaust with its long nickel pipe, the chain-drive transmission, and a host of other mechanical parts."

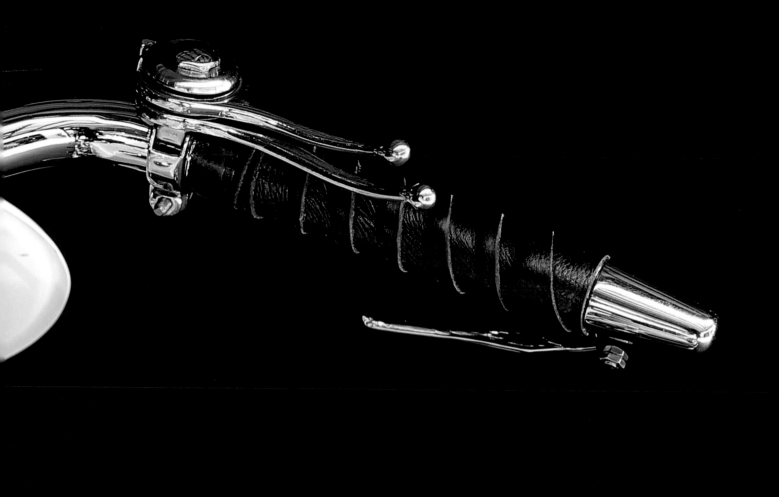
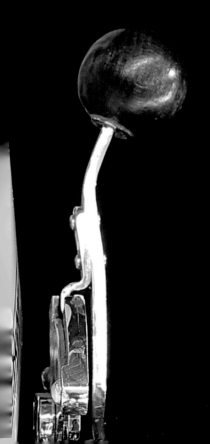

**NICKNAMED "THE BLUE ROCKET,"
THIS MOTORCYCLE IS A MECHANICAL WONDER
THAT COMBINES A CLASSY LOOK WITH
REVOLUTIONARY TECHNICAL ADVANCEMENTS.**

A distinguishing feature of the 1922 Henderson DeLuxe is the speedometer attached to the side of the new gas tank. A flexible cable connects it to a sprocket on the rear wheel.

In 1911, the brothers William and Thomas Henderson, who worked at the Winton Motor Carriage Company cofounded by their grandfather, started developing a revolutionary motorcycle. That same year, they founded their own firm—Henderson Motorcycle Company—and their first model left the factory in Detroit. It featured a 934 cc (57 cu in) four-cylinder engine with belt-drive transmission, fitted with a starter system controlled by a retractable lever attached to the side of the bike.

The two brothers achieved glory in 1912, when the rider Carl Stearns Clancy completed the first round-the-world motorcycle trip riding a Henderson Four. Consequently, the brand shifted focus to specialize in twenty-four-hour endurance races, then in speedway competitions. After World War I, the Hendersons sold the company to Schwinn, the manufacturer of Excelsior motorbikes, and production was moved to Excelsior Motor Manufacturing & Supply Company in Chicago.

The 1920s would mark the peak of Henderson's success—a golden age when its motorcycles rivaled the very best in the world. In 1922, the amazing Series 20 1000 cc Model DeLuxe, one of the finest Excelsior-Henderson bikes, was launched. Equipped with a brand-new gas tank, a saddle mounted on a shock absorber, a double telescopic fork, a cylinder cooling system, and a more powerful rear brake, this speed machine easily exceeded 60 mph and was, for several years, the uncontested queen of the Tacoma Speedway. Note the elegant cylindrical copper speedometer (attached to the side of the gas tank), which was connected to a sprocket on the rear wheel by a flexible cable. The stock market crash of 1929, followed by the Great Depression of the early 1930s, sent the manufacturer—one of the most inventive of this era—into terminal decline. The Blue Rocket remains a star of classic motorcycle rallies and concours d'elegance, its sublime round copper headlight advancing like the prow of a ship.

Manufacturer: Excelsior
Year of production: 1922

Type: V-twin, four-stroke, air-cooled
Displacement: 1,000 cc (61 cu in)
Power: approx. 28 hp
Ignition: Bosch
Clutch: pedal
Secondary transmission: chain
Gearbox: three-speed
Maximum speed: 60 mph

Frame: steel, tubular, single "keystone" cradle (uses the engine as a stressed member)
Suspension: telescopic front fork, rigid rear
Brakes: rear drum brake
Weight: approx. 485 lbs

WF SPORT 600cc

1922

HARLEY-DAVIDSON

COMPANY

Original

A HARLEY-DAVIDSON WITH A CURIOUSLY BRITISH FEEL TO IT, THIS MOTORCYCLE WAS CLEARLY AN ATTEMPT BY THE MILWAUKEE MANUFACTURER TO SMASH THE LIMITS OF POWER AND SPEED IN THE RACING WORLD.

Unearthed by Serge Bueno at a collector's in northern France, this WF Sport was in a pitiful state but was restored to its previous majesty in the Heroes Motors shop.

t was in 1919 that Harley-Davidson decided to accelerate its entry into the racing and speed world at any price. The engineers conceived a motorcycle whose unusual engine and look were inspired by the British Douglas. The Model W—also known as the Sport Twin—featured a 584 cc (35.65 cu in) "boxer" engine—so-called because of its horizontally opposed cylinders—and was equipped with electric ignition. It gained acclaim by breaking an array of speed records and winning long-distance races, including the famous Three Flags Run from Canada to Mexico. The victorious rider, H. C. "Hap" Scherer, a Harley champion of such "long runs," distinguished himself by recording one of the best ever times in the event.

The Models W and WF, which were original, light, and high-performance machines, marked a true turning point in the natural evolution of the motorcycle. Aside from the curious, lengthways-set twin-cylinder engine (with air cooling), this completely restored WF Sport had a number of interesting technological additions. The very long inlet and exhaust manifolds noticeably improved the combustion. The transmission chain was protected by a cover. In another intriguing aspect of the overall aesthetic, the various components of the front fork were fitted with small connecting rods.

There are other details of this WF model that make it stand out from other models: the housing beneath the saddle intended to hold the battery to power the lights, larger tires than on traditional models, the fixed pannier rack, the big headlight, and the length and thickness of the handlebars. But despite its sporting achievements, this sleek machine built for high-performance racing—a Harley-Davidson unlike any other—did not prove popular with American customers. Production of the Models W and WF ceased in 1923.

MODEL J 1000 cc

1922

HARLEY-DAVIDSON

COMPANY

Original

FOLLOWING ITS DEVELOPMENT OF THE V-TWIN ENGINE, HARLEY-DAVIDSON CONTINUED ITS TECHNOLOGICAL ADVANCEMENT WITH THE BIG V-TWIN, WHICH EQUIPPED THE HIGH-END MODEL J AND MODEL JD MOTORCYCLES. THESE TWO BIKES ENCAPSULATED THE IMAGE OF THE BRAND.

The 1922 Model J is instantly recognizable from the toolbox fixed to the top of the gas tank and the horn placed beneath the headlight.

The Model J was promoted by Harley-Davidson as the crème de la crème of large-engined machines. Indeed, the brand used this motorcycle in all of its advertising campaigns, which were designed by the greatest artists of the time. With the rise of the first motorcycle gangs and speed demons, Harley emphasized quiet roads, family, and "bringing people together," an outlook that the brand still promotes today. Harley even launched a magazine (*Harley-Davidson Enthusiast*) in 1916 with a view to cementing its customer base and keeping them informed.

In 1922, the ever-evolving Harley launched the Model JD, fitted not with a 1,000 cc (61 cu in) twin-cylinder engine, but a 1,200 cc (74 cu in) one. This F-head had a record power development of 18 horsepower, ushering in the era of high-powered engines that allowed the mounting of a sidecar. The Model J became the ideal showcase for Harley, due to its look, robustness, and performance. Its engine design was the result of all the technological advances tested during World War I. Featuring a full set of electrical equipment and other details that stood out, this motorcycle, which was rightly considered to be at the top of the Harley-Davidson range, definitely made its mark. A square toolbox was attached to the top of the front end of the gas tank, the large headlight was slightly raised to make room for the horn, and the new, more enveloping mudguard gave the machine a more modern look.

Some accessories, such as the pannier rack, were sold as options, and customers could choose between three tire brands: Firestone, Goodyear, or BFGoodrich. The model shown here, which Serge Bueno bought in a pitiful state at a German motorcycle show, required weeks of work: "Everything was twisted, rusted, or dented. Only the box for tools, gloves, or a sandwich—depending on your preference—was intact. I stuck with it because, in my view, this particular model heralded the future reign of Harley-Davidson. The engineers were wise enough to perfect their Big V-twins instead of succumbing to the siren call of the fuller and more powerful four-cylinder engine."

Type: V-twin, four-stroke, air-cooled, F-head
Displacement: 1,000 cc (61 cu in)
Power: 18 hp
Carburetor: Schebler
Ignition: battery/coil
Transmission: chain
(primary and secondary)
Gearbox: three-speed
Maximum speed: 70 mph

BIKE

Frame: steel, single cradle
Suspension: leaf spring front fork, rigid rear
Brakes: rear drum brake
Weight: 365 lbs

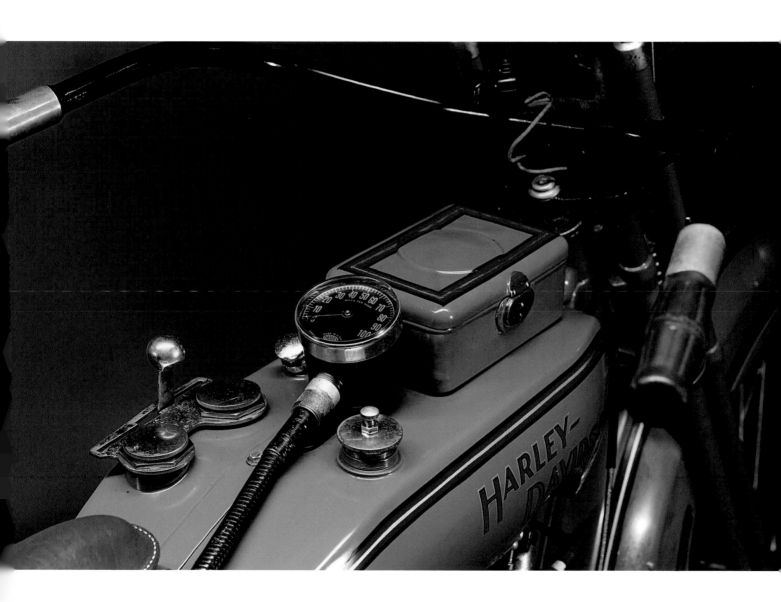

BIG TWIN MODEL CHICAGO

— 1923 —

HARLEY-DAVIDSON

COMPANY

Original

ON JUNE 26, 1915, CHICAGO'S SPEEDWAY PARK OPENED, USHERING IN A NEW ERA AND STYLE OF COMPETITION THAT WOULD SEE MOTORCYCLES RACE EVEN FASTER.

The Chicago model was a picture of impressive efficiency: no suspension, no brakes, no mudguards. Lightness and power were all that mattered.

The speedway could hold nearly 80,000 spectators. Its architecture and its elongated oval design would become the benchmark for all other racetracks in the United States. Despite fierce competition, Chicago would come to hold a unique place in the hearts of the public, the motorcycle manufacturers, and the riders. It was a symbolic showcase, and a win here at any price was a must. This was the sole reason Harley-Davidson produced the Chicago model, a vertiginous competition motorcycle intended to thrash its rivals.

In the speedster world, this monster was also nicknamed—quite rightly—"The Suicide Machine." It was propelled by the brand's recently developed Big Twin engine (1,000 cc/61 cu in) and had neither suspension nor brakes, which partly explains the high number of fatalities associated with it—both riders and spectators. "This exceptionally high-performance machine quickly earned itself a reputation as an indomitable motorcycle and the legend has endured," explains Serge Bueno. "For me, the Chicago is pure rawness and efficiency. A sniper bullet. The pinnacle of speed. The rider lay atop the gas tank, his hands glued to the dropped handlebars. I hunted for this treasure for years before I found it, in an abysmal state, and I had to source a number of parts from various places. I worked incredibly hard on its restoration, feeling it come back to life day by day. I took particular care with the paintwork because I wanted a deep color; finding the right patina was a delicate process. This is a work of mechanical art different from the others, because it excels in its simplicity and the cleanness of its lines."

Manufacturer: Harley-Davidson
Year of production: 1922

Type: V-twin, four-stroke, air-cooled
Displacement: 1,000 cc (61 cu in)
Power: 20 hp
Carburetor: Schebler
Gearbox: none
Transmission: chain
Maximum speed: 120 mph

Frame: steel, loop
Suspension: none
Brakes: none
Weight: 240 lbs

FOR HARD-CORE DEVOTEES OF MAGNAT-DEBON —
"THE FIRST TOURING BRAND" ACCORDING TO
ONE OF ITS SLOGANS—THE SADLY LITTLE-KNOWN
BMSC 350 CC DELUXE REMAINS A CULT MOTORCYCLE.
ITS METICULOUS DESIGN, SLEEK LINES, AND ADVANCED
TECHNOLOGY MAKE IT A DREAM MACHINE.

The art of the classic French motorcycle: a symphony of copper, cables, and reworked colors that form a flashy, hyperrealist picture.

fter World War I, the American military left behind a considerable stock of Harley-Davidsons and Indians. These high-performance motorcycles, hitherto never seen in Europe, were extremely popular and sold for much less than those already on the European market. The French manufacturers therefore had to adapt in order to rival them not only in price, but also in mechanical enhancements. The Magnat-Debon 350 cc Deluxe, considered a high-end touring motorcycle, benefited from the technical progress made with the old sports models and the brand's latest innovations.

The engine remained the same—a 350 cc (21.35 cu in) four-stroke with side valves—as did the overall philosophy of the machine. But there were additions of a front drum brake and an acetylene canister fixed below the seat to supply the copper headlight. The shaft of the engine lubrication pump, sticking up from the side of the gas tank, was longer, too—another improvement—but otherwise this was a traditional Magnat-Debon through and through. It even retained its hand-pumped horn.

This motorcycle was a wreck when Serge Bueno came across it—again in the Lyon area. "Like the other sports model featured, the whole restoration took me more than three weeks. This time, I refined the finish of the paintwork even more, since it required two different hues plus the pin-striping. By chance, at a flea market, I found a palette of colors used by the brand that year (1925). It was a real treat detailing the range of synthetic varnishes and cellulose-based lacquers. So I worked up patinas of old burgundies, oranges, and yellow."

3270 VH73

SIDE-VALVE
1926
TERROT
DIJON

TERROT, THE MARKET LEADER IN FRANCE, CONTINUED TO PROGRESS DURING THE 1920S. ITS ENGINEERS UNVEILED NEW MOTORCYCLE MODELS AT THE PARIS MOTOR SHOW IN 1925, INCLUDING THE HT 350 CC, WHICH BOASTED A NUMBER OF MECHANICAL IMPROVEMENTS.

Restored to its original look, using period parts sourced from all over the world—such as the speedometer and the gas tank cap—this Terrot HT 350 has an edgy presence.

In the eyes of purists, the Type H undoubtedly remains Terrot's major success. It was the same for the public, who appreciated the variations of this model (HT, HS, and HTC, the extra initials standing for "Tourist," "Sport," and "Comfort," respectively). The top-of-the-range of the 1926 season remains this Supersport motorcycle and its four-stroke 350 cc (21.35 cu in) JAP engine. It is a highly seductive machine, with an aluminum piston, an open exhaust, a three-speed gearbox, chain-cum-belt transmission, separate oil tank and mechanical pump, hub brakes, and, above all, the eagerly anticipated appearance of the Druid fork, the old style having long had its day. From 1927, adjustable shock absorbers and a manual oil pump (controlled from the handlebars) were also added.

Photographed three-quarters on, against a black background, with the mudguard removed from the fat front tire, the glove/toolbox fixed on top of the gas tank, and its impressive engine, this motorcycle looks a little like a contemporary custom bike. "I wanted it to retain its forbidding, aggressive, 'racing' look," admits Serge Bueno. "And I restored it with that in mind. When I arrived in the United States, my greatest pleasure was to introduce Americans to the incredible talent and ingenuity of our French motorcycle engineers in the interwar period. Winning over Californians, who have been immersed in this bike culture since forever gave me an intense joy. Later on, when museums—such the Haas Moto Museum in Dallas—began exhibiting my eye-catching French motorcycles, I knew that I had realized my childhood dream."

Manufacturer: Terrot
Years of production: 1926–28

Type: single-cylinder vertical (JAP), four-stroke, air-cooled
Displacement: 350 cc (21.35 cu in)
Power: approx. 13 hp
Carburetor: Amal
Secondary transmission: chain
Gearbox: three-speed
Maximum speed: 60 mph

BIKE

Frame: steel, single "keystone" cradle (uses the engine as a stressed member)
Suspension: Druid type parallelogram front fork, rigid rear
Brakes: drum (front and rear)
Weight: 240 lbs

UP UNTIL 1925, THE PEUGEOT CATALOGUE
CONTAINED ONLY MOTORCYCLES OF QUITE AVERAGE
PERFORMANCE—175 CC (10.7 CU IN) AND 250 CC
(15.25 CU IN). WITH THE P104, WHICH WAS
SHOWCASED AT THE PARIS MOTOR SHOW
IN OCTOBER 1926, THE LION BRAND BARED
ITS CLAWS. A NEW CONTENDER HAD ARRIVED.

With this P104, the venerable lion brand announced its arrival. The addition of the rev counter and speedometer only served to enhance the elegance of this French classic.

Below: One of Peugeot's advertising posters.

Developed by Peugeot to compete with Terrot, its legendary rival, this magnificent P104 certainly had a wonderful appearance for the period. In addition to its beautiful lines and classy look, the machine also featured some interesting technical and mechanical innovations, such as a new 350 cc (21.35 cu in) four-stroke engine with side valves, and a sprung front suspension. There were some very clever details, such as the two-in-one rev counter and speedometer connected to the universal joint of the front wheel, the rearview mirror, and the headlight powered by a dynamo.

Other components improved the machine's modernity and style further still, such as the two sheet-metal skirts to protect the rider's legs, the toolbox fixed to the top of the gas tank, the wide, spring-mounted seat made of soft leather, and the leather pouch hung on the pannier rack. The fat tires and wide mudguards added to the "new look" of this elegant machine. This motorcycle was manufactured until 1928, when it was superseded by the P107.

Serge Bueno bought this P104 from a French collector who had maintained his motorcycle well. "It gives me enormous pleasure to meet enthusiasts who take care of their machines to keep the memory alive. Very often, the owners of such museum pieces don't want to part with them, but they know me by reputation and trust me to take their motorcycles and enhance them. In this particular case, I undertook only a light restoration and a new paint job in period colors."

Manufacturer: Peugeot
Years of production: 1926–28

ENGINE

Type: single-cylinder, four-stroke, air-cooled, side-valve
Displacement: 350 cc (21.35 cu in)
Power: approx. 8 hp
Clutch: metal-on-metal cone
Gearbox: three-speed
Secondary transmission: chain
Maximum speed: approx. 50 mph

BIKE

Frame: steel, double cradle
Suspension: parallelogram sprung front fork with adjustable shock absorbers, rigid rear
Brakes: drum (front and rear)
Weight: 285 lbs

MONET-GOYON
CORPORATION
— MC SPORT DELUXE 350 cc —
1926

IN APRIL 1917, IN DIJON, FRANCE, ENGINEER JOSEPH MONET AND FINANCIER ADRIEN GOYON FOUNDED THEIR COMPANY AS WORLD WAR I RAGED ON. THEY INVENTED THE VÉLOCIMANE, A KIND OF TRICYCLE POWERED BY THE ARMS, TO BE USED BY WOUNDED AND DISABLED SOLDIERS FROM THE CONFLICT. NEXT THEY TRANSITIONED TO PRODUCING HIGH-SPEED MOTORCYCLES.

A beautiful, classic French bike in all its shining splendor, rebuilt with passion by Heroes Motors down to the tiniest of details, such as leaving the "hairs" on the clincher tires (a result of the rubber molding process) and the American and French flags that decorate the tip of the front mudguard (below).

The ZS, a sporty 175 cc (10.7 cu in) model, won numerous titles, including Speed French Champion, and took the world speed record in 1924. Two years later, Monet-Goyon launched its MC Sport Deluxe, which was equipped with a four-stroke 350 cc (21.35 cu in) MAG engine with opposing valves. This motorcycle, which deserves to rank high in the hit parade of beautiful French bikes, was extremely sophisticated. The three-speed gearbox was controlled by an elegant lever placed to the right of the gas tank. Funnily enough, this gear lever was made by the British firm Burman.

Serge Bueno fell in love with this motorcycle, or rather what was left of it, at a flea market in central France during one of his long scouting expeditions. "It was, and I choose my words carefully, a wreck when I found it. What caught my eye was the dynamo, a quite specific type, connected to the rear wheel, which powered the Luxor headlight. I then sourced spare parts in various states of disrepair. I had to piece together the puzzle, manufacture the missing parts, and completely redo the engine. It was a complete restoration job, taking six weeks, which also involved remaking the kick starter, the quick release mechanism for the wheels, the front drum brake, the front fork with parallelogram suspension, and the clincher tires. Then there was the famous rear mudguard decorated with the American and French flags—a nod to this motorcycle with a Swiss engine and British gears: a 'world bike' before its time!"

Year of production: 1926

Type: single-cylinder (MAG), four-stroke, air-cooled

Displacement: 350 cc (21.35 cu in)

Power: 8 hp

Transmission: chain (primary and secondary)

Gearbox: three-speed, manual shifter

Maximum speed: approx. 55 mph

Frame: steel, tubular, double "keystone" cradle (uses the engine as a stressed member)

Suspension: parallelogram front fork, rigid rear

Brakes: front drum brake

Weight: approx. 265 lbs

BMW
R 47

500 cc

MANUFACTURED FOR ONLY TWO YEARS
(1927–28), BMW'S R47 WAS A VERY SPORTY,
HIGH-POWERED MACHINE. ITS REFINED DESIGN
AND CLASS STILL MAKE THIS MOTORCYCLE
A QUEEN OF THE CONCOURS D'ELÉGANCE.

With its triangular copper speedometer and the leather strap and cap surround on the second gas tank, this motorcycle would look right at home in your living room.

Right: The BMW workshop, which was already synonymous with perfection.

Equipped with a 500 cc (30.5 cu in) longitudinal boxer engine (the crankshaft was mounted along the transmission axis), a universal joint, and a frame connected directly to the steering and the rear axle, developing 18 horsepower and yet weighing just 287 lbs (130 kg), this stupendous machine could reach 70 mph. The BMW engineers designed this motorcycle along the same lines as the R37 and R32 models; the steel tubular frame had no rear suspension and the front fork used leaf springs.

Fewer than 1,700 units of this gem were produced, making it a rare motorcycle of great interest to collectors. The R47 was sold with a large number of options. Headlights, horn, speedometer, and pillion—none were included as standard. Neither was the second gas tank, which was attached to the main tank with a stylish brown leather strap in perfect harmony with the bike's sleek lines.

For Serge Bueno, this BMW is a splendor: "As is often the case, I unearthed this R47 after arriving at a German motorcycle show at dawn. It was in a deplorable state, all in pieces. But I have always considered this model to be synonymous with a work of art. It has a wild elegance, very haute couture. It was a real delight to bring it back to life. It is testimony to a unique craftsmanship."

Manufacturer: BMW
Years of production: 1927–28

Type: boxer longitudinal, four-stroke, air-cooled
Displacement: 350 cc (21.35 cu in)
Power: 18 hp
Gearbox: three-speed
Secondary transmission: shaft
Maximum speed: 70 mph

BIKE

Frame: steel, tubular, double cradle
Suspension: plate spring front fork, rigid rear
Brakes: front drum brake, rear block brake
Weight: 285 lbs

The R47 photographed
from the front: you can
really sense the power
of the boxer engine.

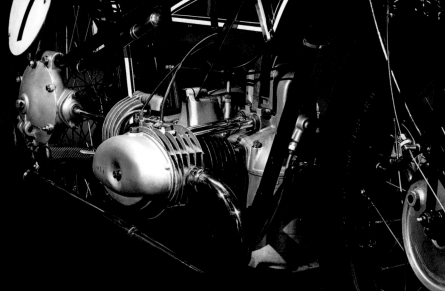

500 NS SPORT

1927

TERROT

DIJON

IN 1927, THE STRATEGISTS AT TERROT, WHOSE WORKSHOPS WERE LOCATED ON RUE ANDRÉ COLOMBAN IN DIJON, MADE A BIG SPLASH BY PRODUCING A HIGH-END SERIES THAT THEY CALLED THE 500S.

Out of the many marvels that Serge Bueno has restored in his Heroes Motors shop, this Terrot 500 NS Sport features in the top five of his personal hit parade.

The famous 500 Blackburne series (NMT, NMS, NMSS, among others) became the star motorcycles of 1928, but one of Terrot's masterpieces remains the 500 NS Sport, whose avant-garde design, mechanical innovations, and performances were every bit as good as American motorcycles. This is yet another classic example of mechanical art made in France.

Terrot had to have its own 5 horsepower motorcycle, and it produced one with panache. The 500 NS Sport was a significant step-up, featuring a host of new and extraordinary technologies. The motorcycle was equipped with a four-stroke JAP engine, a three-speed gearbox, twin exhaust, eight-inch hub brakes, a Druid type fork with adjustable shock absorbers, fat tires, and many other important details that made this machine extremely desirable.

In addition to the 2.11 gallon (8 liter) gas tank (later increased to 3.43 gallons/13 liters), there was a reserve tank located in a leather pouch attached to the pannier rack. The 0.4 gallon (1.5 liter) oil tank (later increased to 0.63 gallon/2.4 liters) was fitted with a mechanical pump and an auxiliary hand pump; as if that were not enough, a backup oil can was attached to the front fork. The cylindrical copper speedometer was connected directly to the front wheel axle by a cable. There was a choice of Terry or Lycett saddle, both spring-mounted. Last but not least, the toolbox was placed within reach of the rider, on top of the gas tank.

"It looks as if everything on this dream machine was meticulously well thought out," says Serge Bueno. "The Americans didn't invent the motorcycle, the French did. Motorcycle manufacturing in France is full of marvels, including this crazy Terrot that took me weeks to restore to its original state. I sometimes even slept in my shop to gain more time to work on it."

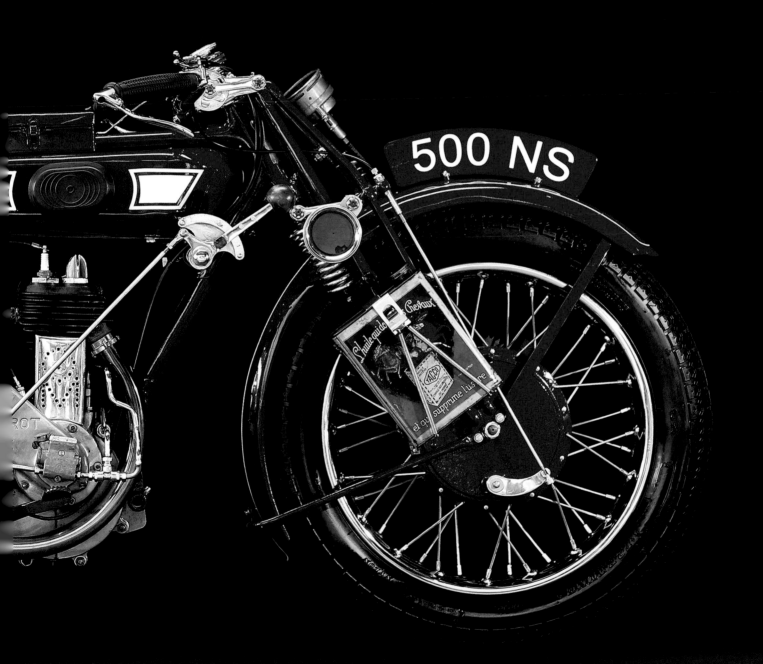

The perfection of the details only adds to the already considerable reputation of this beautiful machine: toolbox, stamped with the Terrot logo, fitted to the top of the gas tank; backup oil can attached to the front fork with bungee cord; and simple yet stylish speedometer.

Manufacturer: Terrot
Year of production: 1927

Type: single-cylinder (Terrot-JAP),
four-stroke, air-cooled, side-valve

Displacement: 500 cc (30.5 cu in)

Power: approx. 18 hp

Gearbox: three-speed

Transmission: chain (primary
and secondary)

Maximum speed: Approx. 60 mph

Frame: steel, single "keystone" cradle
(uses the engine as a stressed member)

Suspension: Druid type parallelogram
front fork, rigid rear

Brakes: drum (front and rear)

Weight: approx. 285 lbs

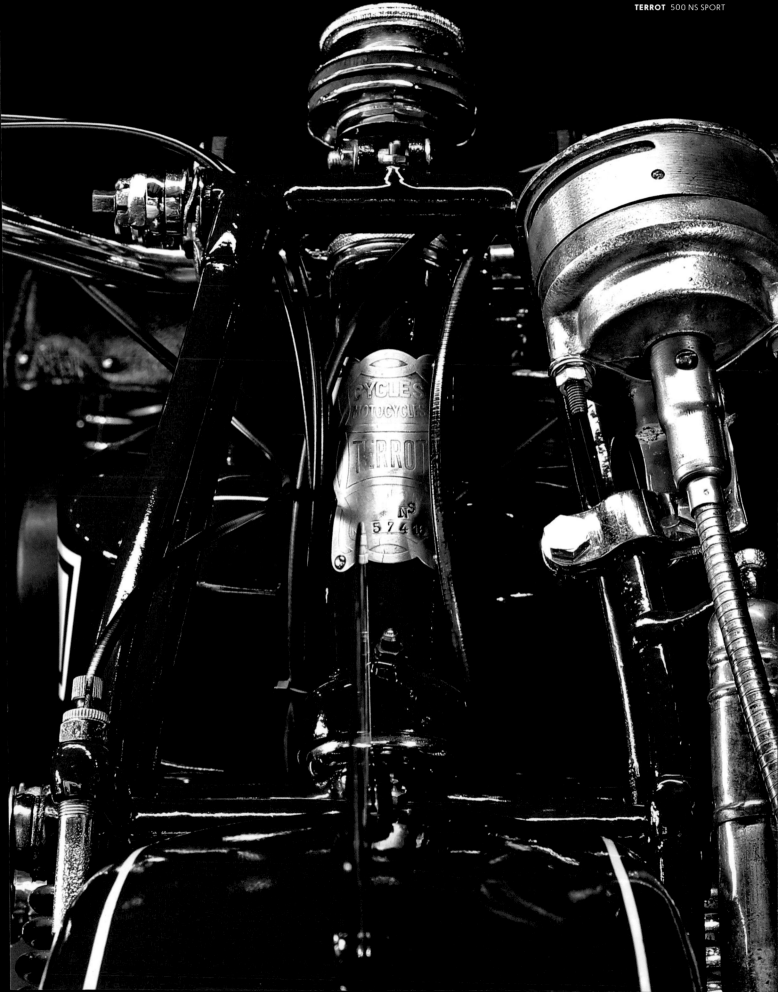

Designed by Marcel Dumont, this 23T was conceived for adventure. It was restored to its original state, down to the smallest details, from the speedometer to the rider number.

I n interwar Europe, long-distance motorcycle races were very popular with the general public and served as test beds for the major brands to prove the reliability of their engines and tires. From 1921, Saroléa started manufacturing striking motorcycles fitted with chain-drive transmissions. The machines sold well in Europe and even in markets as far away as Japan. Renowned in the world of racing, speed, and long-distance endurance rallies, Saroléa hit a high point in 1928 with the production of the 23T, a model equipped with a 500 cc (30.5 cu in) flat engine. This was a key year for the brand, which stopped producing the "flat tanker," and pioneered a highly effective front braking system.

The Saroléa 500 cc 23T seen here was completely rebuilt by Serge Bueno, who was able to give this motorcycle back its adventurous look and the feel of a long-range endurance machine.

"A good collector is a lucky collector, and I must admit that I am often spoiled," says Serge. "I found this motorcycle in scattered parts at the premises of a guy who was a real enthusiast of the brand. I completely overhauled it from A to Z: the engine, the transmission, the carburetor, the magneto-dynamo system, the brakes, the tires, and the spokes. At another sale I had bought a load of documentations, drawings, and photographs concerning this indefatigable beast, which enabled me to reconstruct it precisely. The saddlery part was essential: the two leather pouches—front and rear, fixed to the mudguards—as well as the belt around the gas tank, also in leather, comprising three pouches for tools, gloves, and provisions. I then sourced and restored the additional gas tank that attached to the pannier rack with two leather straps. In 2015, this motorcycle left the Heroes Motors workshop to take part in the Vintage Revival Montlhéry. It was totally at home among the other queens of mechanical wonder from this grand era."

Manufacturer: Saroléa
Year of production: 1928

ENGINE

Type: single-cylinder, four-stroke, air-cooled, overhead valve
Displacement: 500 cc (30.5 cu in)
Power: approx. 18 hp
Ignition: magneto-dynamo
Secondary transmission: chain
Gearbox: three-speed, manual shifter
Maximum speed: 70 mph

BIKE

Frame: steel, single open cradle
Suspension: Druid type parallelogram front fork, rigid rear
Brakes: drum (front and rear)
Weight: approx. 230 lbs

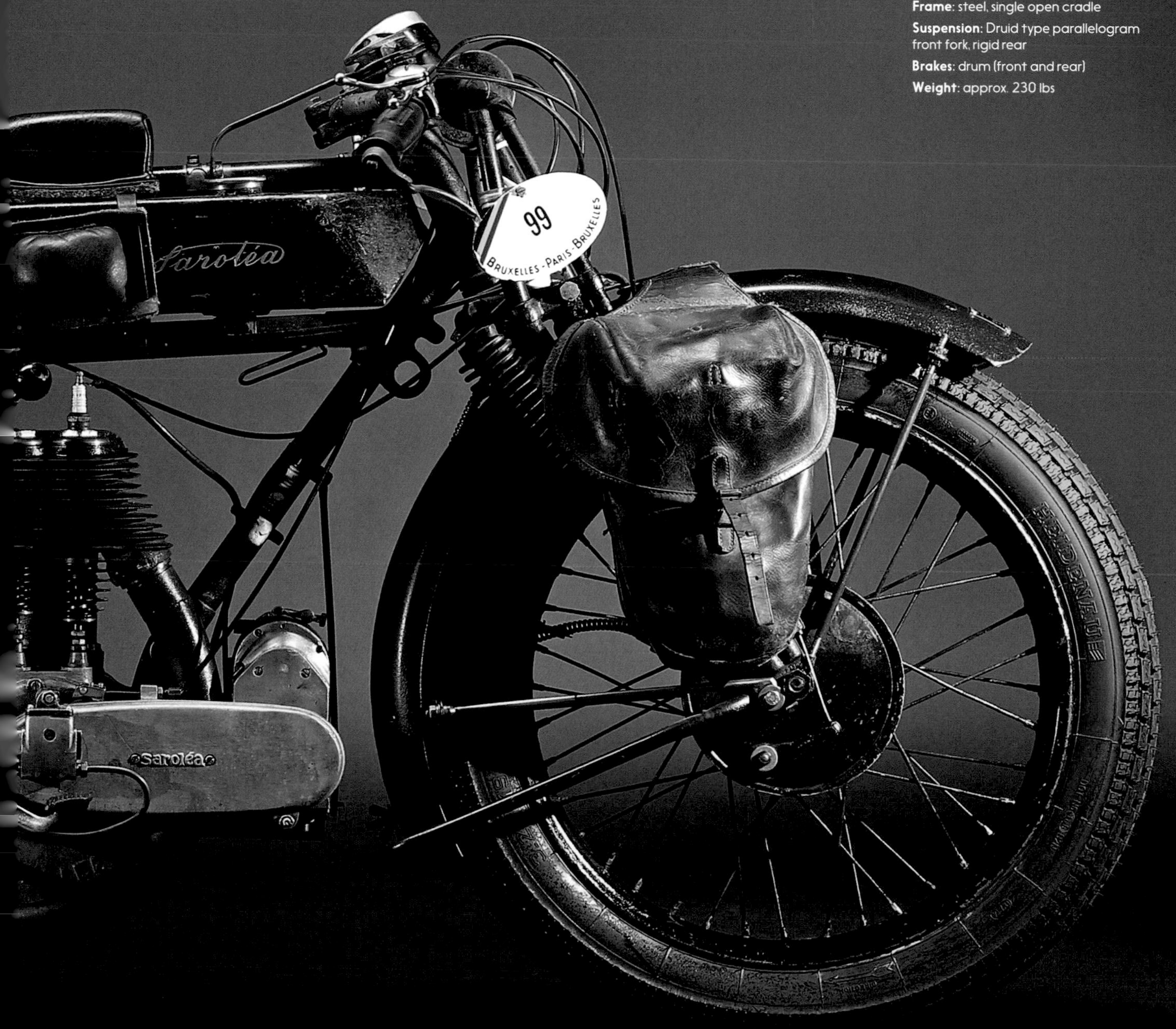

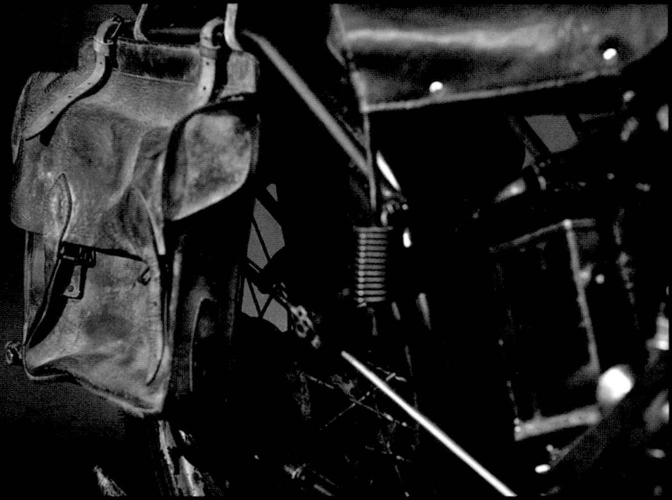

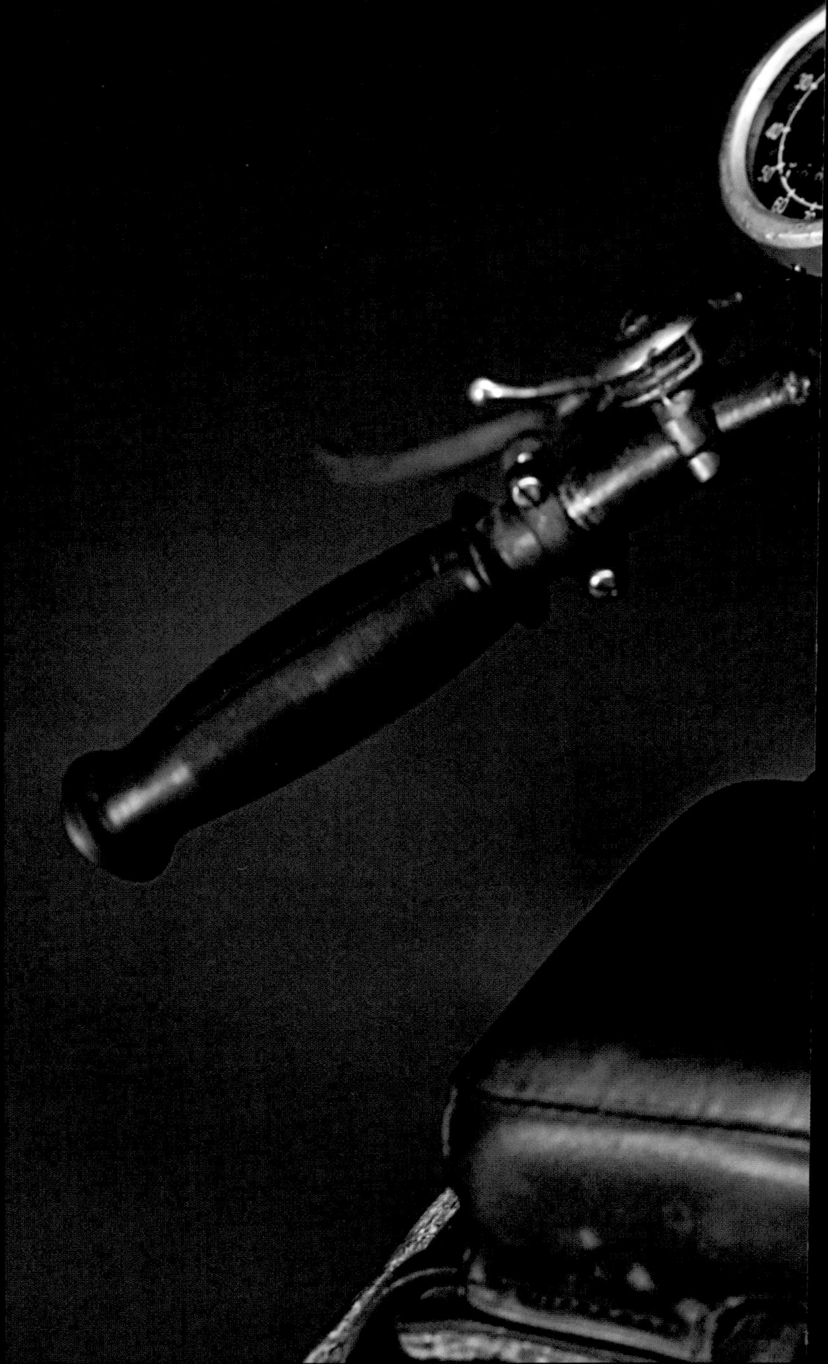

GILLET HERSTAL, THE BELGIAN MOTORCYCLE AND CAR MANUFACTURER BASED IN HERSTAL, STARTED PRODUCTION IN 1919, AND BECAME WORLD-FAMOUS WHEN TWO OF ITS RIDERS COMPLETED A CIRCUMNAVIGATION OF THE GLOBE ON GILLET HERSTAL 350S.

How can you not be awed by this design, where the shine of the copper and steel propel you into a world of mechanical artistry?

June 14, 1926, is an important date in the history of the motorcycle. On that day, Robert Sexé and Henri Andrieux set out from Paris by motorcycle to attempt a round-the-world ride. Sexé was no novice; a motorcyclist, photographer, and globe-trotter, he had already undertaken many extreme long-distance motorcycle trips. This new challenge was a success: 22,000 miles covered in a little less than six months, via Japan and the United States, where the two adventurers met several future star riders. With this epic trip Gillet Herstal entered the pantheon of legendary motorcycles.

This 1928 Sport Rallye was a worthy heir to the bike used on the round-the-world trip. The simplicity of this tourer, built for devouring very long mileages, was deceptive. This light motorcycle (210 lbs/95 kg) had all the qualities of a winner. It was equipped with a sturdy little 350 cc (21.35 cu in) engine, an Amac carburetor, and a chain-drive transmission. Its most distinctive feature was the braking system: pads on the front wheel and a drum on the rear, offering the rider a significant degree of safety. The front suspension, of the girder type, also provided greater comfort to the rider, as did the wide soft-leather seat, which was mounted on springs. In another nod to comfort, two small leather cushions were fixed to the sides of the gas tank to protect the knees. The copper headlight and the small leather tool pouch rounded off the look of this sophisticated, understated adventurer.

"I am a fanatical admirer of this breed of exceptional motorcycles—sometimes unknown to the general public—which have marked the history of this passionate sport," Serge Bueno professes. "I was incredibly lucky to find this jewel practically in its original state in Belgium. A light restoration was sufficient to rejuvenate it and return it to its former luster. The bike certainly deserved it!"

Manufacturer: Gillet Herstal
Years of production: 1925–28

ENGINE

Type: single-cylinder, two-stroke, air-cooled
Displacement: 350 cc (21.35 cu in)
Power: approx. 10 hp
Carburetor: Amac
Gearbox: two-speed
Secondary transmission: chain
Maximum speed: 55 mph

BIKE

Frame: steel, single "keystone" cradle (uses the engine as a stressed member)
Suspension: parallelogram front fork, rigid rear
Brakes: front block brake, rear drum brake
Weight: 210 lbs

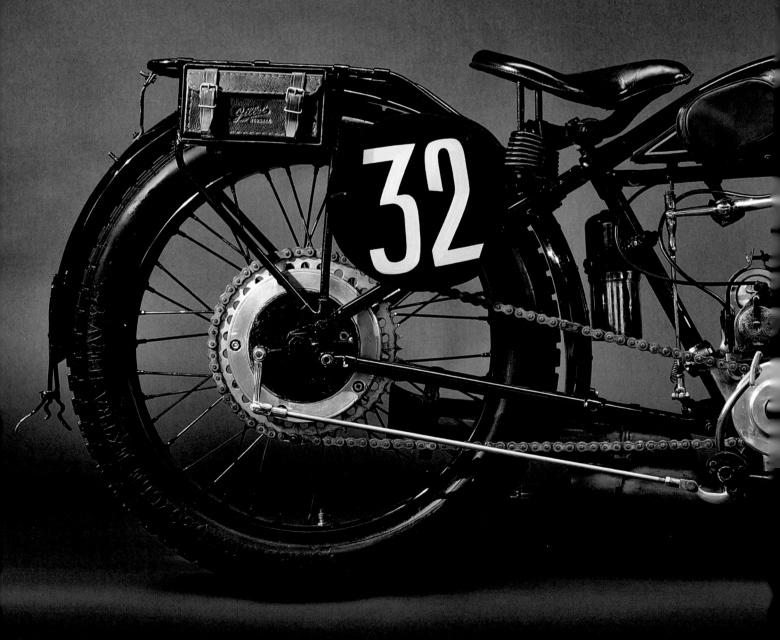

Gillet
HERSTAL

1928

GILLET WAS NOT CONTENT WITH PRODUCING EXCEPTIONAL ROAD MACHINES DESIGNED SPECIFICALLY FOR LONG-DISTANCE RALLIES. THIS SUPERB MANUFACTURER ALSO MADE ITS MARK ON PURE SPEED RACES WITH THIS MONSTER: THE GILLET HERSTAL 500 SUPERSPORT.

This champion of the racetracks and breaker of speed records received a new lease on life in the Heroes Motors shop.

For two years in succession, the Belgian rider Victor Vroonen won the prestigious French endurance race, the Bol d'Or, astride a Gillet Herstal 500 Supersport and forever enshrined this superlative racing machine in motorcycling history. At the finish, Vroonen declared to the waiting press, "I felt like I was riding an untamed mustang." Indeed, his wild horse attained 90 mph.

The Gillet Herstal 500 Supersport was like dynamite on the racetracks. Its engine block—a Gillet single-cylinder four-stroke with tappet valves—was so tall that the riders dubbed it the "cathedral engine." Nothing was left to chance. The rocker arm shafts, for example, were fitted inside tubes, themselves covered by aluminum cases. The other technical specs were also impressive: cylinder head in two parts fixed directly to the casing; magneto ignition; three-speed, multidisc gearbox with lever-operated shifter located on the front right of the gas tank; twin exhaust; parallelogram front fork; 170 mm (6.69 in) drum brakes at the front and rear; and high-pressure tires. This was a heavy beast (175 kg/385.8 lbs), but it flew like a rocket.

Serge Bueno still recalls this purchase: "It was a miraculous discovery. I acquired this extremely rare and exceptional motorcycle from a Belgian collector, who had pampered it all his life. It was in perfect condition. It is no easy thing to sell collectors' motorcycles because there are some true experts out there. You need to have real specimens with full pedigrees. You need excellence. This machine here is reserved for the rarest of purists."

Manufacturer: Gillet Herstal
Year of production: 1929

Type: single-cylinder, four-stroke, air-cooled, overhead valve
Displacement: 500 cc (30.5 cu in)
Power: 24 hp
Ignition: magneto
Gearbox: three-speed, manual shifter
Transmission: shaft (primary), chain (secondary)
Maximum speed: 80 mph

BIKE

Frame: steel, single cradle
Suspension: parallelogram front fork, rigid rear
Brakes: drum (front and rear)
Weight: 375 lbs

19❦29
MAJESTIC
500 CC

WHEN GEORGE ROY DREAMED UP THIS LEGENDARY
FRENCH MOTORCYCLE, MANUFACTURED IN 1929,
HE HAD IN MIND A COMBINATION OF THE BEST
FEATURES OF AN AUTOMOBILE AND A BIKE—
SOMETHING HE WAS SURE WOULD STAND OUT
FROM THE MACHINES BEING PRODUCED BY OTHER
MANUFACTURERS. THE CHASSIS—COMPOSED OF TWO
LONGERONS—AND THE ENGINE WERE CONCEALED
BY A METAL BODY PANEL. THE MAJESTIC WAS ALSO
ONE OF THE FIRST MOTORCYCLES TO USE HUB-CENTER
STEERING. CONSIDERED TOO REVOLUTIONARY FOR
ITS TIME, ONLY ONE HUNDRED OF THESE MAGNIFICENT
MACHINES WERE EVER PRODUCED, ONE OF WHICH
WAS ACQUIRED BY THE BUENO FAMILY.

Half-motorcycle/half
car, the Majestic's highly
sophisticated dashboard has
four dials: a speedometer/
odometer, a fuel gauge,
an oil gauge, and a clock.

Right: an advertisement
from the period.

In 2016, Bobby Haas, a customer of Heroes Motors and the owner of the
Haas Moto Museum in Dallas, bought this rarity from Serge Bueno and made
it one of the centerpieces of his museum. Serge set to work and the great
saga of the Majestic's renaissance began.

Serge knew that the restoration of this antique would take several months,
so he devoted himself to this challenge full-time. But first he had to ship the
contraption (disassembled and in multiple boxes) from France to his shop
in Los Angeles. "When it arrived," Serge recalls, "I realized that I only had 90
percent of the bike; missing were the nuts and bolts, the cables, the saddle, the tires, and a few parts of
the dashboard. The only solution
was to buy original parts, which
are very hard to find, at the
Veterama show that takes place
in Germany every October. So I
only really began the restoration
on November 16, 2015, which is a
date impossible for me to forget
because it's my father's birthday."

The first stage involved
inspecting the chassis and the
wheel alignment and replacing rusted parts. It was quite complicated to
get the Majestic back on its two wheels, in view of the particularities of
this half-car/half-motorcycle. Next Serge tackled the engine. It took him
120 hours of meticulous work to replace the bearings and some internal
parts and then mount it on the chassis. Once the motorcycle was complete, he disassembled it and sent the parts to a specialist in Downtown
Los Angeles for nickel-plating. Meanwhile, he worked on everything to do

with the bodywork, before the painting stage. Serge opted for red, since that was the color the 1929 Majestic models were painted (the 1930 models were painted blue). All that was left was to redo the wheel spokes. Three weeks later, all of the separate parts were delivered to Heroes Motors, freshly nickel-plated, and Serge began reassembling the now gleaming Majestic: "That process took me another two weeks. Then, finally, I could take it out for a ride beneath the California sun, cruising through Beverly Hills on this ninety-year-old motorcycle."

Mission accomplished, after five months of dogged work and the pride of having achieved the impossible! If you are passing through Dallas, you can admire this red beauty at the Haas Moto Museum.

Manufacturer: Majestic
Year of production: 1929

ENGINE

Type: single-cylinder (Chaise), four-stroke,
air-cooled, overhead valve

Power: 11 hp

Ignition: magneto

Clutch: multiple disc in oil bath

Transmission: shaft (primary),
chain or universal joint (secondary)

Gearbox: three-speed, manual shifter

Maximum speed: 60 mph

BIKE

Frame: two longerons covered
with a metal body panel

Suspension: front sliding pillar
with hub-center steering, rigid rear

Brakes: drum (front and rear)

Weight: 330 lbs

T Sport Rallye

NSU
MOTORENWERKE AG

Side-Valve 350cc
═ 1929 ═

THIS GERMAN MANUFACTURER, FOUNDED BY
CHRISTIAN SCHMIDT IN NECKARSULM IN 1873,
ORIGINALLY SPECIALIZED IN THE PRODUCTION
OF KNITTING MACHINES. IN 1886, NSU STARTED
MANUFACTURING BICYCLES, THEN MOTORCYCLES
IN 1901, AND FINALLY AUTOMOBILES IN 1905.

The highly distinctive front of the classy NSU Model T Sport. Its round, chromed headlight—powered by an ingenious acetylene gas system—adds to the charm of this German beauty.

NSU had a prosperous year in 1929, and the firm hired Walter William Moore, the famous engineer and designer who is considered the father of the Norton International. Arriving in Germany from Birmingham, England, Moore completely shook up NSU, breathing new and redeeming life into the company. This Model T Sport made its remarkable appearance on the German market in 1929, soon followed by the European debut. Aesthetically speaking, this was a sleek, harmonious, and elegant machine. The wide, enveloping mudguards on both the front and rear wheels gave it an interesting avant-garde look. Fitted with a 350 cc (21.35 cu in) side-valve engine, front drum brake, fishtail exhaust pipe, and a parallelogram suspension, this motorcycle was unique in that the brake and gearshift controls were reversed. The round, chrome-plated headlight was powered by an acetylene system attached to the frame. The discreet manual oil pump was fixed to the side of the gas tank.

"I was fortunate enough to pick up this machine in Germany in a decent state, requiring only a partial restoration," says Serge Bueno. "In cases such as these, I love perfecting the paintwork—using the cellulose lacquers of the period—getting the patinas and the thin lines in different colors just right. Because all motorcycle photography at the time was in black and white, the use of thin golden lines on a dark-colored motorcycle brought out the shape of the machine." This German beauty is sure to be a star at any concours d'elegance.

Manufacturer: NSU
Year of production: 1929

Type: single-cylinder four-stroke, air-cooled, side-valve
Displacement: 350 cc (21.35 cu in)
Power: approx. 12 hp
Secondary transmission: chain
Gearbox: three-speed, manual shifter
Maximum speed: approx. 60 mph

Frame: steel, single cradle
Suspension: parallelogram front fork, rigid rear
Brakes: front drum brake
Weight: approx. 200 lbs

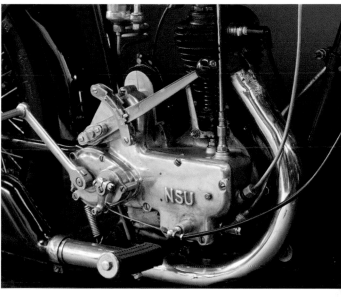

HST 350 SIDE-VALVE

1929

TERROT

DIJON

FROM 1929 TO 1932, WITH THE GREAT DEPRESSION IN FULL SWING, TERROT KEPT ITS FOOT ON THE GAS AND PRODUCED ITS STANDARD MODEL, HST—THE MOTORCYCLE FOR WHICH IT WOULD BECOME KNOWN.

The beauty of this copper headlight, which used acetylene gas, illustrates how the Terrot craftsmen paid careful attention to detail.

With this superb machine—unveiled at the Paris Motor Show of 1929—we see all the craftsmanship of the French technicians of this "quality brand" (one of Terrot's slogans). The advertising placed in the special Paris Motor Show issue of *Moto Revue* met with great success. The HTS was fitted with a four-stroke, 350 cc (21.35 cu in) side-valve engine. The frame hung low and the front part was made of brazed tubes. The Druid parallelogram fork and the friction shock absorbers were both adjustable, as were the handlebars.

"I found this motorcycle in the South of France in good condition, which is very rare," confides Serge Bueno. "Its owner had taken the greatest care of it so I only did a light restoration. The large copper head-light (acetylene) was intact. I simply had to service the electrical parts—lights, horn, dynamo, and battery—and the mechanical lubrication system, change the little rubber pad fixed to the side of the reservoir for knee protection, the leather of the sprung saddle, and the leather pannier hung on the tubular rack."

The HST, which could reach over 55 mph, also had a three-speed gearbox—suspended from the rear fork—incorporating three cork discs and five steel discs. This was a light, classy, and relatively fast motorcycle that became a showcase for Terrot. Lovingly maintained and lightly restored with passion by Heroes Motors, this machine is a homage to mechanical greatness.

Manufacturer: Terrot

Years of production: 1930–31

ENGINE

Type: single-cylinder, four-stroke, air-cooled, side-valve

Displacement: 350 cc (21.35 cu in)

Power: approx. 10 hp

Carburetor: Amal or Gurtner

Transmission: chain (primary and secondary)

Gearbox: three-speed

Maximum speed: 60 mph

BIKE

Frame: steel, single "keystone" cradle (uses the engine as a stressed member)

Suspension: Druid type parallelogram front fork with adjustable shock absorbers, rigid rear

Brakes: drum (front and rear)

Weight: approx. 265 lbs

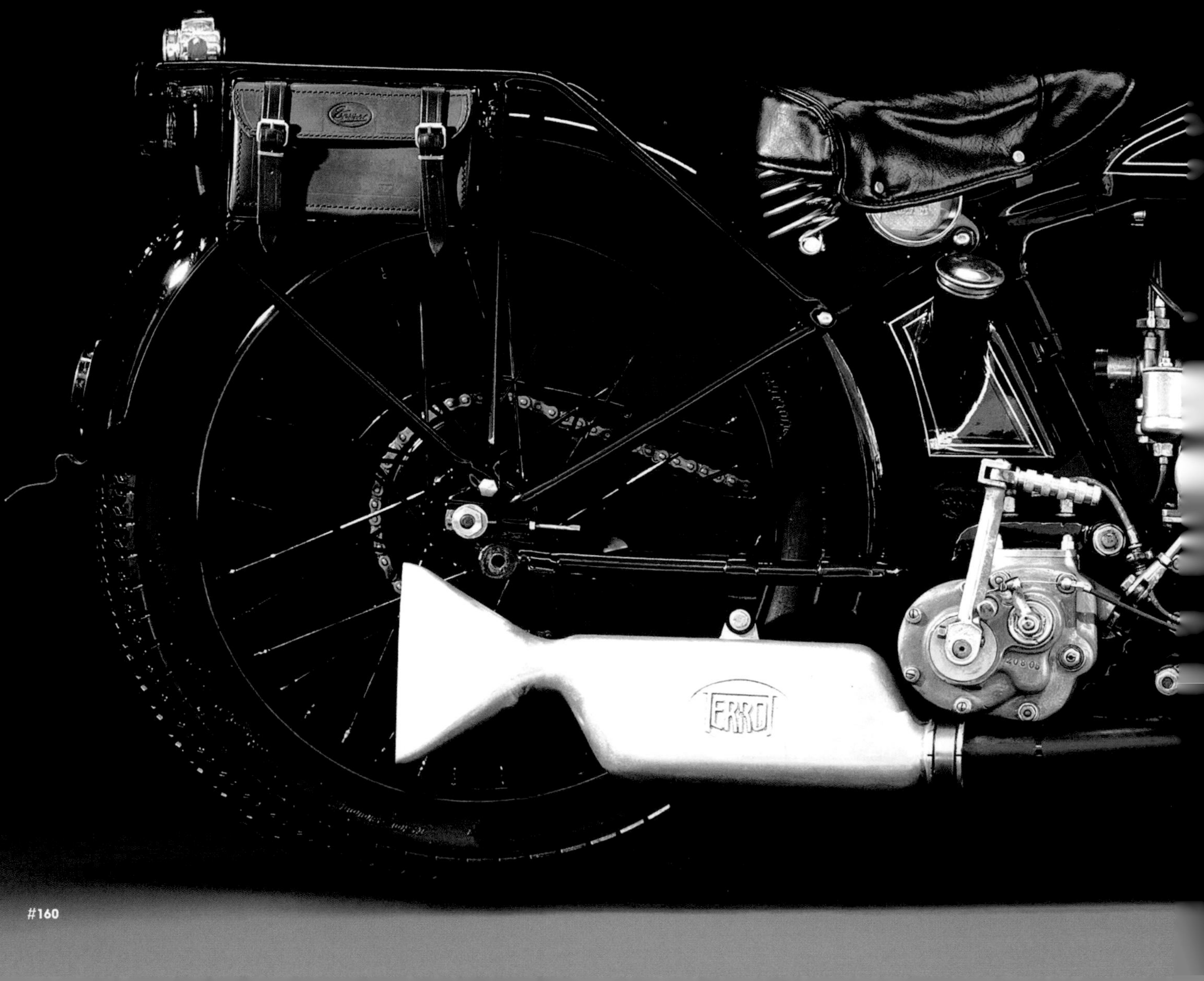

Above and right: A French beauty that wears its ninety years with pride, from the pump horn to the metal toolbox, and the little leather pouch.

Opposite: The perfect aesthetics of a mechanical art from the interwar period.

FN
M67
RACER
1930

THE BELGIAN COMPANY FABRIQUE NATIONALE (FN), BASED IN HERSTAL, WAS ORIGINALLY AN ARMS MANUFACTURER. IT ONLY BEGAN MAKING MOTORCYCLES IN 1901. THREE YEARS LATER, AT THE PARIS MOTOR SHOW, FN LAUNCHED A STRIKING HIGH-PERFORMANCE MACHINE WITH A FOUR-CYLINDER IN-LINE ENGINE DISPLACING 362 CC (22.1 CU IN).

In the late 1920s, the FN 500 cc was dubbed "the fastest single-cylinder in the world."

After World War I, FN produced the M Series—a new range of high-quality single-cylinder motorcycles with side valves—which was really successful in Europe. The 1930 FN M67 was a worthy heir to this famous M Series. With its single-cylinder, four-stroke, side-valve F-head engine displacing 500 cc (30.5 cu in), the M67 performed beautifully on hill climbs, mountain races, and long-distance rides. This machine was up there with the best motorcycles of its generation. It was equipped with a chain-drive transmission, a three-speed gearbox with hand shifter, a Druid parallelogram front suspension, and drum brakes at the front and rear. Finally, the rocker arms and the rods were protected, and the cylinder-head attachments were reinforced. This M67 Factory Racer had the hallmark of being fitted with a new, larger gas tank and two Waymaster fat tires.

"I found the owner of this motorcycle through the intermediary of an enthusiast of the brand," Serge Bueno recalls. "At one point, I thought I would completely restore it, but I realized that I preferred it in its original state. I think it has an incredible look, a bit like those customized dirt bikes. There is something 'mean' about it, with that fat front tire and no mudguard. This machine participated in the Hand-Shifter-Run, a race that takes place in the Austrian Alps, at an altitude of over 8,200 feet."

Manufacturer: FN
Year of production: 1930

ENGINE

Type: single-cylinder, four-stroke, air-cooled, side-valve

Displacement: 500 cc (30.5 cu in)

Power: 12 hp

Carburetor: Amal (bronze)

Transmission: chain (primary and secondary)

Gearbox: three-speed, manual shifter

Maximum speed: approx. 80 mph

BIKE

Frame: steel, double cradle

Suspension: Druid type parallelogram front fork, rigid rear

Brakes: drum (front and rear)

Weight: approx. 240 lbs

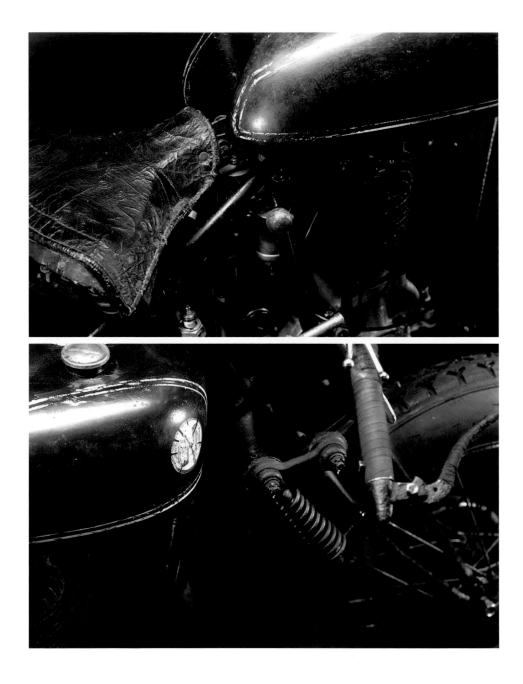

MONET-GOYON
CORPORATION
— RACER SUPERSPORT 500 cc —
1930

VIRTUALLY UNKNOWN TO THE GENERAL PUBLIC BUT VENERATED BY A HANDFUL OF AFICIONADOS, THIS IS ONE OF THE GREAT FRENCH MOTORCYCLES. SERGE BUENO HIMSELF AFFIRMS THAT THIS SUBLIME MACHINE IS "THE MOTORCYCLE OF A LIFETIME."

Close-up of the gas tank and handlebars of this stunner, which still stirs the fantasies of the most hardcore enthusiasts.

"I have spent a chunk of my life searching for that rare gem: an exceptional motorcycle that you simply fall in love with at first glance," Serge Bueno says. "There were wonderful Harley-Davidsons and Indians, then that red, stream-lined 1929 Majestic. But this 1930 Monet-Goyon 500 cc Racer Supersport was on a whole other level. It is a little-known and extremely rare museum piece, appreciated only by a select band of enthusiasts, great connoisseurs, and passionate collectors. It's almost a spiritual thing, 'shamanic' even, that I just can't explain. It's a feeling you get when you set eyes on it for the first time." Serge bought this gem from an especially meticulous French collector. The founder of Heroes Motors and the 500 Racer were clearly destined to find each other.

This Monet-Goyon was originally a racing version of the 1928 H Series, revised by the engineer Raymond Guiguet for the Grand Prix de Montlhéry. Everything was designed for speed: the huge four-stroke, 500 cc (30.5 cu in) MAG engine with hairpin valve springs, the transmission, the Villers carbure-tor (which was boosted), the high-compression piston, the double oil pump to lubricate the high-performance cylinder, and the reinforced gas tank. There were also the parallelogram fork and the little leather cushion located behind the saddle for a more aerodynamic prone riding position. To save weight, the protective cover of the drive chain was even perforated to make it lighter. The result was a motorcycle that would not look out of place in *Mad Max*.

Manufacturer: Monet-Goyon
Year of production: 1930

ENGINE

Type: single-cylinder (MAG), four-stroke, air-cooled, high-compression piston, double oil pump
Displacement: 500 cc (30.5 cu in)
Power: approx. 18 hp
Carburetor: Gurtner M26 with separate oil reservoir
Secondary transmission: chain
Gearbox: three-speed, manual shifter
Maximum speed: approx. 95 mph

BIKE

Frame: steel, double cradle
Suspension: parallelogram front fork, rigid rear
Brakes: drum (front and rear)
Weight: approx. 240 lbs

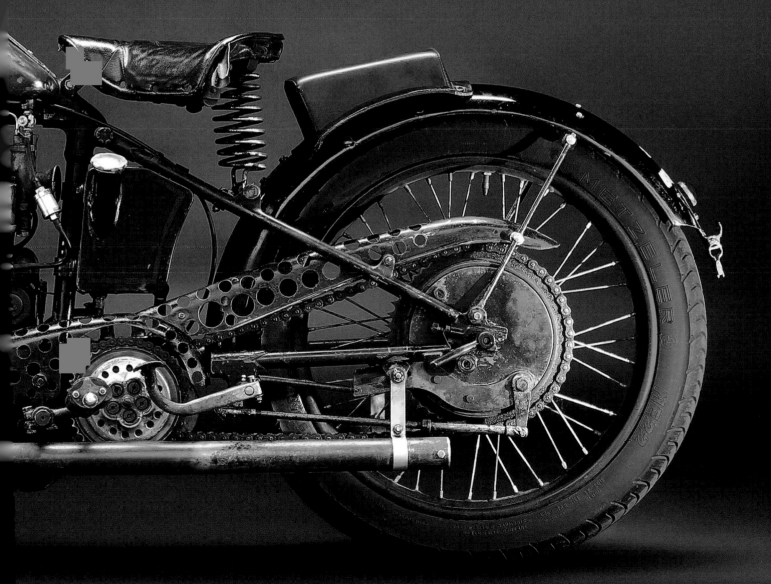

FOUNDED IN 1902, THE BICYCLE MANUFACTURER GRIFFON ALSO PRODUCED MOTORCYCLES RIGHT FROM THE START. BY 1904, GRIFFON BIKES WERE GETTING ATTENTION IN THE SPORTS WORLD, NOTCHING UP ONE SUCCESS AFTER ANOTHER IN VARIOUS COMPETITIONS, PARTICULARLY THE CLIMB OF MONT VENTOUX IN THE SOUTH OF FRANCE. IN 1919, GRIFFON JOINED THE LA SPORTIVE CONSORTIUM THAT COMPRISED SEVERAL BRANDS, INCLUDING PEUGEOT. THEN THE "DRAGON BRAND" LAUNCHED THE G505S, A LUXURY TOURING MOTORCYCLE, IN 1929.

The Griffon, with its additional oil tank—pumped manually—fixed to the gas tank.

This beautiful French machine had an excellent reputation; it was sturdy, as easy to ride as it was to maintain, and had a modern, elegant look. Equipped with a four-stroke, side-valve engine displacing 350 cc (21.35 cu in), the G505s bore a strong resemblance to the Peugeot P108 (250 cc/15.25 cu in). This 1931 model was fitted with drum brakes (front and rear), a chain-drive transmission, a three-speed gearbox with manual shifter, and front suspension. The oil pump for lubricating the engine was fixed to the gas tank. The fine, little leather tool bag placed on the pannier rack and the oil can attached with bungee cord by the rear wheel made this motorcycle classier still. The spring-mounted saddle was a perfect extension of the gas tank—painted red and black—making the motorcycle appear even more aerodynamic.

"I unearthed this motorcycle at a market in the South of France," says Serge Bueno. "It was in a halfway decent state, but still required a partial restoration of the mechanics and a touch-up of the paintwork. I had to source the chain guard as well as the speedometer and the cable connecting it to the front wheel. You should also know that the large headlight was sold separately, as an option. In short, a really beautiful piece that fit perfectly in my catalogue."

Frame: steel, single "keystone" cradle
(uses the engine as a stressed member)

Suspension: parallelogram front fork,
rigid rear

Brakes: drum (front and rear)

Weight: approx. 265 lbs.

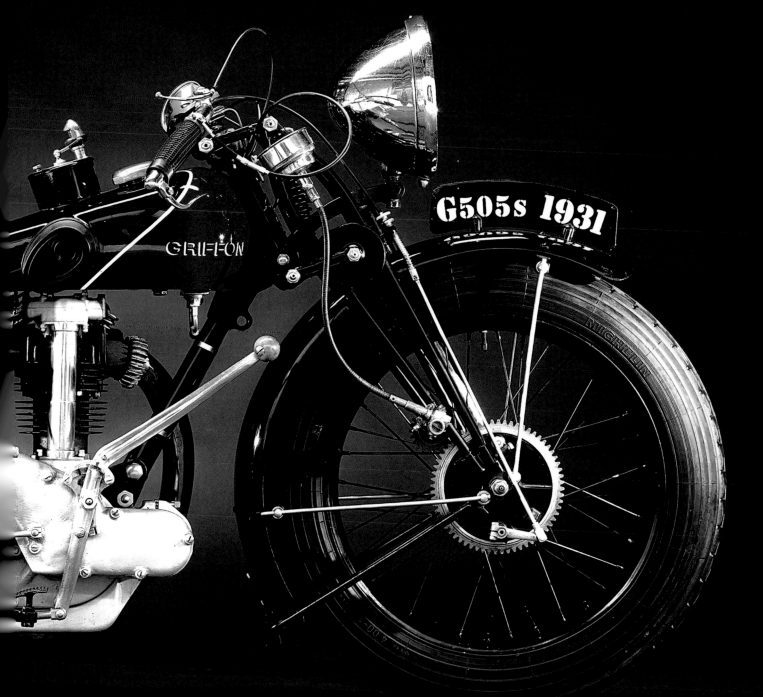

GRIFFON

G505s 1931

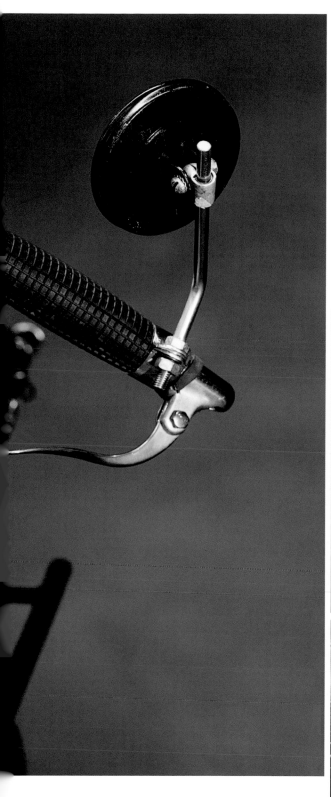

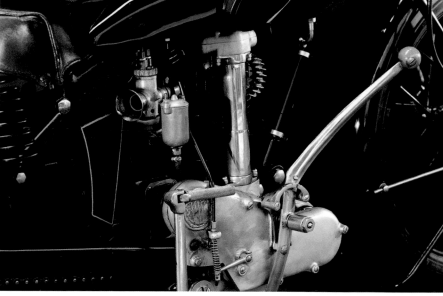

GNOME & RHÔNE

· 1933 ·

CM1 350 cc

IN 1915, THE COMPANIES GNOME AND LE RHÔNE MERGED AND THE RESULTING GNOME ET RHÔNE BECAME THE LEADING AIRCRAFT ENGINE MANUFACTURER. AT THE END OF WORLD WAR I, THE COMPANY BOUGHT THE LICENSE TO THE BRITISH MOTORCYCLE BRAND ABC AND STARTED MAKING MOTORCYCLES.

Produced to expand the range of Gnome et Rhône motorcycles, the CM1 kept every one of its promises and still remains an exceptional machine that is highly sought after by collectors.

Produced in 1920, the first Gnome et Rhône, the Type A, had a flat twin-cylinder engine and front and rear suspension. It was followed over the next few years by the Type D, Type E, and Type M. This magnificent CM1 from 1933 is a rare model that Serge Bueno has completely restored. "There are certain meetings that are unforgettable—moments of pure magic," Serge remembers. "I found this beauty at a fair in the South of France. It was in a pitiful state, all in pieces. I had to redo everything from A to Z: the engine, the mechanics, and the paintwork. It took me three weeks. The very day that I finished the restoration, an enthusiastic client came and bought it from me."

This bike was a splendidly seductive beast, combining aesthetics, elegance, and performance, and featuring what is known as a "cathedral" engine design, along with the latest French sophistications of that wonderful interwar period. The four-stroke, single-cylinder pushrod engine (displacing 350 cc/21.35 cu in) was very tall—like that of the Gillet Herstal—hence the "cathedral" nickname. Nothing was left out: a three-speed gearbox with a manual shifter located beside the gas tank, drum brakes at both the front and rear, drive chain covered by a metal guard, and a fishtail exhaust pipe. The fat tires, the saddle placed in a continuous line with the gas tank, the leather pad fixed to the rear mudguard—to enable the more aerodynamic prone riding position—and the raised taillight all added to the class of this work of art.

Manufacturer: Gnome et Rhône
Year of production: 1933

Type: single-cylinder, four-stroke, air-cooled
Displacement: 350 cc (21.35 cu in)
Power: approx. 10 hp
Ignition: magneto
Secondary transmission: chain
Gearbox: three-speed, manual shifter
Maximum speed: approx. 60 mph

Frame: steel, double cradle
Suspension: parallelogram front fork
Brakes: drum (front and rear)
Weight: approx. 265 lbs

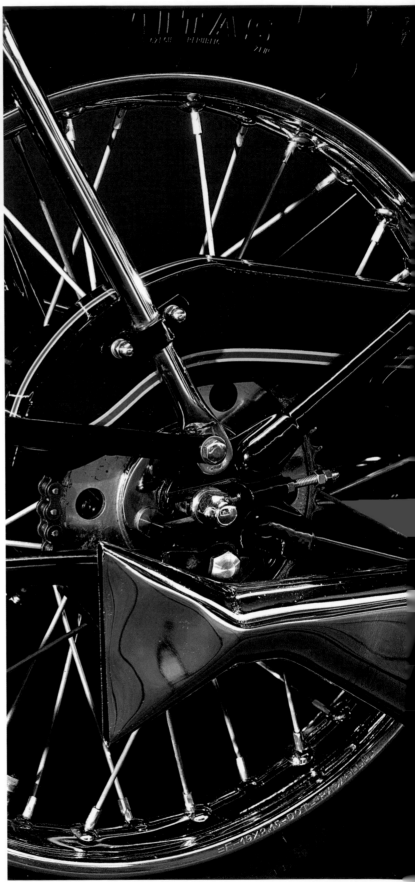

THE MANX GRAND PRIX IS A SPEED RACE THAT HA[S] TAKEN PLACE ON THE ROADS OF THE ISLE OF MAN SINCE 1923, ALONGSIDE THE FAMOUS TOURIST TROPHY. VICTORY AT ONE OF THESE COMPETITION[S] WAS HIGH RECOGNITION FOR A RIDER AND A MANUFACTURER. IN 1936, EXCELSIOR TOOK UP THE CHALLENGE.

A very special motorcycle built for an even more special race on the Isle of Man, in the Irish Sea.

This Excelsior Manxman was the fruit of a collaboration between the engineer and designer H. J. Hatch and Eric Walker, who both worked for the Excelsior Motor Company in Birmingham, England. Excelsior was already known for its 1933 Marvel model (as in "mechanical marvel"), whose twin-camshaft engine was built by Blackburne. In 1936, Excelsior started building its own engines.

The 1936 Excelsior Manxman was fitted with a two-valve, single overhead camshaft engine displacing 250 cc (15.25 cu in). It had a four-speed gearbox, chain-drive transmission, girder front forks, and drum brakes. The machine weighed just 287 lbs (130 kg), but could reach over 80 mph.

In 1936, Henry Tyrell-Smith, one of Excelsior's two racers, placed second in the Lightweight category of the TT race, while the other, Denis Parkinson, won the Manx Grand Prix, also on a Manxman.

"I found this Excelsior Manxman in Germany in practically its original state, and I only had to do a little light restoration here and there," says Serge Bueno. "It was important to me to own these heroines of the Isle of Man races, particularly since Denis Parkinson won the Manx Grand Prix on one of these bikes."

Manufacturer: Excelsior
Year of production: 1936

Type: single-cylinder, four-stroke, overhead camshaft, air-cooled
Displacement: 250 cc (15.25 cu in)
Power: 23 hp
Carburetor: Amal TT
Secondary transmission: chain
Gearbox: four-speed, pedal shifter
Maximum speed: 82 mph

BIKE

Frame: steel, single cradle
Suspension: parallelogram front fork, rigid rear
Brakes: drum (front and rear)
Weight: 287 lbs

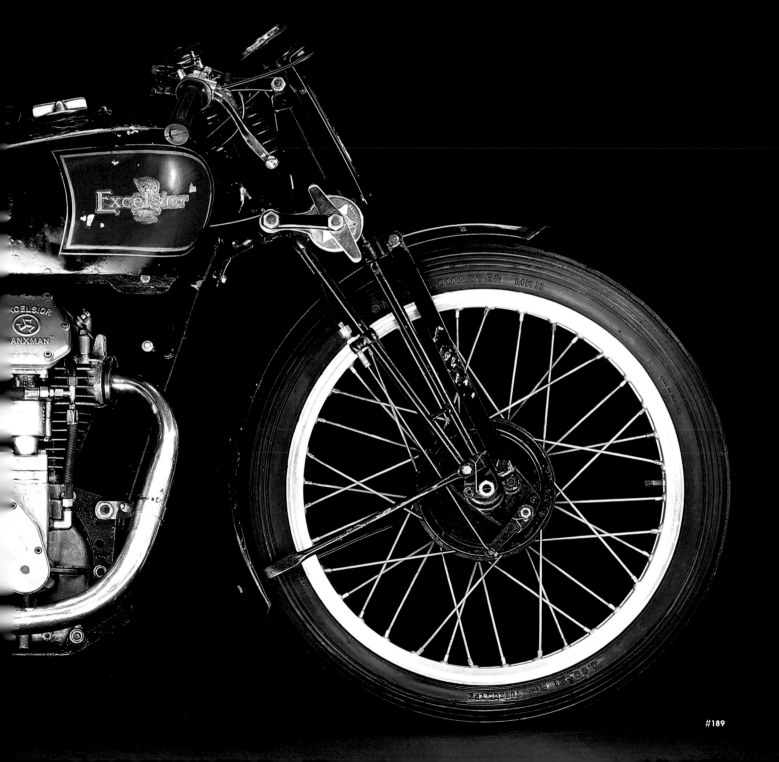

MOTOBALL
– 350 cc –
KOEHLER-ESCOFFIER
1936
*

THE GAME OF MOTOBALL BEGAN IN THE UNITED KINGDOM IN 1923. TWO TEAMS OF SIX PLAYERS FACED OFF AGAINST EACH OTHER ON A STANDARD-SIZED SOCCER PITCH. GAMES COMPRISED TWO FIFTEEN-MINUTE HALVES WITH A FIVE-MINUTE BREAK IN BETWEEN. THE RULES CHANGED LATER, INCREASING THE PLAYING TIME TO FIFTY MINUTES WITH A TEN-MINUTE BREAK. THIS ORIGINAL BUT HIGHLY DANGEROUS SPORT, WHICH WAS SIMILAR TO POLO—WITH HORSES REPLACED BY MOTORCYCLES— SOON TOOK OFF INTERNATIONALLY, BECOMING VERY POPULAR IN FRANCE IN THE EARLY 1930S.

With its front fat tire and no mudguard, this queen of Motoball matches looks like something out of *Mad Max*. Its power, lightness, and maneuverability were a winning combination.

Right: a color period advertisement praising the prowess of this "record-breaking motorcycle."

The most famous French teams were from Dijon, Saint-Étienne, Paris, Nice, Sochaux, Nevers, Avignon, and, above all, Carpentras, whose players rode the famous Koehler-Escoffier, another great French brand, which boasted a 1,000 cc (61 cu in) model.

The 350 cc (21.35 cu in) version seen here was light, powerful, and agile. To keep the bike as lightweight as possible, it had no front mudguard and the gas tank was relatively small. The parallelogram fork and the two studded fat tires proved highly effective for delicate maneuvering.

"Only the two goalies were not on motorcycles," explains Serge Bueno, "and therefore risked fewer injuries. I found this 350 cc (21.35 cu in) model at a collector's in Normandy. It was in a terrible state, but I took great pleasure in bringing it back to life because it was a unique piece with proportions that are quite contemporary. It had remarkable acceleration, even though it could only get up to 30 mph. Another museum piece."

KOEHLER ESCOFFIER
LA MOTO DES RECORDS

Manufacturer: Koehler-Escoffier
Year of production: 1936

Type: single-cylinder, four-stroke, air-cooled
Displacement: 350 cc (21.35 cu in)
Power: 9 hp
Ignition: magneto
Secondary transmission: chain
Gearbox: three-speed, pedal shifter
Maximum speed: 50 mph

Frame: steel, single "keystone" cradle
(uses the engine as a stressed member)
Suspension: parallelogram front fork,
rigid rear
Brakes: drum (front and rear)
Weight: 200 lbs

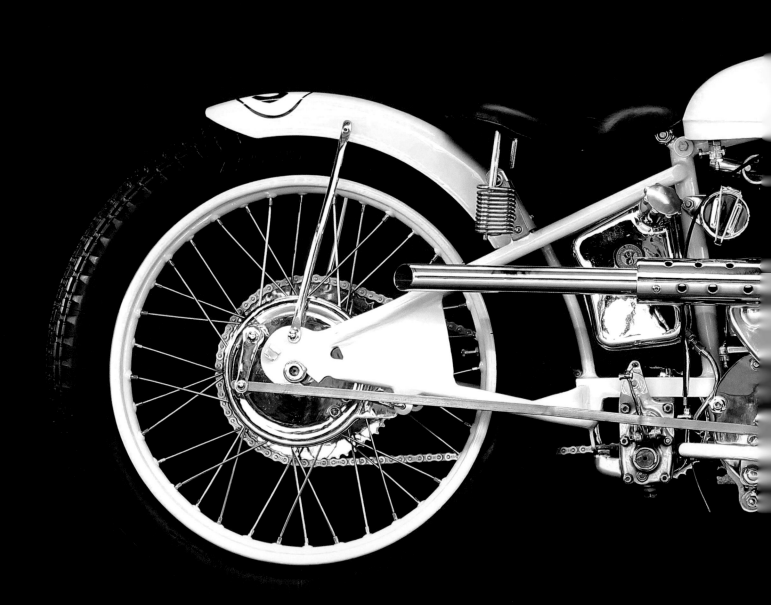

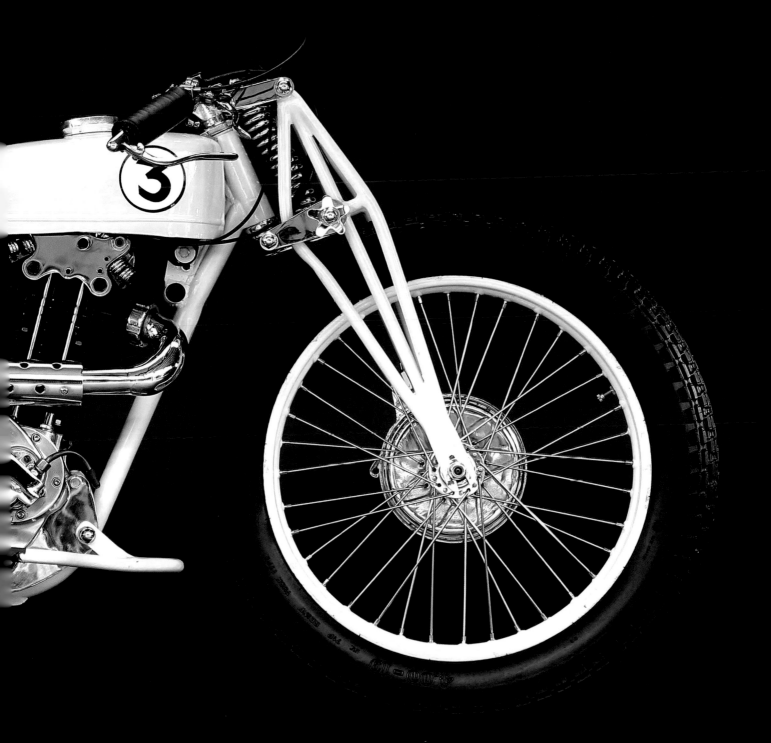

INTERNATIONAL M30
★ ★

Norton

★ 1937 ★

THE 1930S WERE A FANTASTIC PERIOD FOR NORTON'S RACING DEPARTMENT. FROM 1931 TO 1939, ITS MOTORCYCLES AND RIDERS WON THE LEGENDARY ISLE OF MAN TOURIST TROPHY NINE TIMES IN A ROW.

Close-up of the handlebars and speedometer of this speedster: the perfect combination of class and power and the terror of the Tourist Trophy races on the Isle of Man.

T**he** Norton International story began in 1927 when the brilliant Walter William Moore (formerly the chief designer at Douglas) created the first Norton overhead camshaft engine. Several years later, Moore left to join the German company NSU, but his legacy was a series of speedsters that cemented Norton's reputation. This 1937 model was a competition motorcycle fitted with a single-cylinder, four-stroke, double overhead camshaft engine displacing 500 cc (30.5 cu in). This engine could be finely tuned to best suit different racetracks.

The relatively small size of the single-cylinder engine combined with a high-performance frame; modified gas and oil tanks; a conical brake housing, which gave greater stability; and rear plunger suspension made this 500 cc motorcycle the weapon of choice for speed racers. This model went on to win the Tourist Trophy—the craziest and most dangerous race in the world—several times.

The compact yet stylish shape of the Model 30—a powerful little motorcycle if ever there was one—was characteristic of British motorcycle design. The two leather pads—just behind the saddle and on top of the imposing gas tank—allowed the rider to adopt a more aerodynamic prone riding position.

"In my view, the Norton International is a historic motorcycle of the first order in the annals of the Isle of Man Tourist Trophy," claims Serge Bueno. "It also marks the start of an era when British motorcycles ruled the world. I found this 500 cc model in an atrocious state during an unplanned visit to a British fair. It took a considerable amount of work, but I had all the technical manuals and period photographs to help me do the job. And anyway, a machine with such a cult status as this deserves to see the light of day again in all its splendor."

Manufacturer: Norton
Year of production: 1937

Type: single-cylinder, four-stroke, double overhead camshaft, air-cooled
Displacement: 500 cc (30.5 cu in)
Power: 50 hp
Ignition: BTH magneto
Carburetor: Amal
Transmission: chain (primary and secondary)
Gearbox: four-speed, pedal shifter
Maximum speed: 130 mph

Frame: steel, double cradle
Suspension: parallelogram front fork, rear plunger
Brakes: drum (front and rear)
Weight: approx. 320 lbs

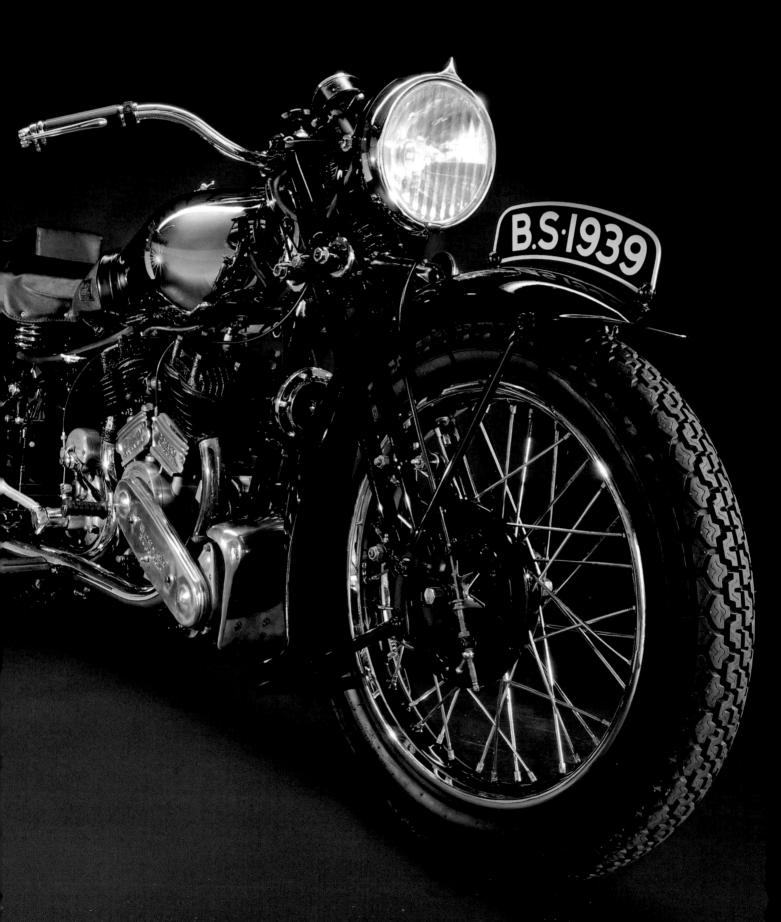

1938
BROUGH SUPERIOR
SS80 1000 cc

IN 1919, THE INDUSTRIALIST GEORGE BROUGH STARTED MANUFACTURING LUXURY MOTORCYCLES AND CARS IN NOTTINGHAM, ENGLAND. THESE SUPERB AND HIGHLY SOPHISTICATED MACHINES WERE THE PRESERVE OF THE RICH ELITE WHO ADORED EXCEPTIONAL MOTORCYCLES.

Right: T. E. Lawrence (of Arabia) on his SS100 with JAP engine—a very expensive dream machine reserved for the elite.

T. E. Lawrence—better known as Lawrence of Arabia—owned seven Brough motorcycles and died after crashing on a 1927 SS100 model. The playwright George Bernard Shaw was also an unconditional devotee of this cult motorcycle, as was the actor Steve McQueen— owner of an enormous collection of classic motorcycles—who had an SS80 that he put up for sale at a concours d'elegance in Pebble Beach, California. According to legend, McQueen lent this bike to his friend Kenneth Howard—the high priest of Kustom Kulture and also known as Von Dutch—for several years. On October 16, 2011, a 1928 SS100 "Moby Dick" model sold for $260,000 at auction. The letters "SS" stood for "Super Sports," while the numbers 80 or 100 indicated maximum speed in miles per hour.

In 1935, Brough equipped the SS80 with a 990 cc (60.41 cu in) Matchless V-twin engine—similar to what Harley-Davidson and Indian were using. (The SS100 model retained its four-cylinder JAP H engine.) It also had a three-speed gearbox. Only four hundred of this Matchless model were produced, which explains its rarity and high prices on the collector's market. The Brough SS80 was a knockout, boasting a very modern design, and it won more than fifty speed races. The visionary manufacturer himself rode an SS80 that he nicknamed "Spit and Polish" in reference to the pristine finish he maintained on the bike.

Years of production: 1935–39

Type: V-twin (Matchless), four-stroke, air-cooled

Displacement: 1,000 cc (61 cu in)

Power: 50 hp

Secondary transmission: chain

Gearbox: four-speed

Maximum speed: 100 mph

BIKE

Frame: steel, single plunger cradle

Suspension: front leading-link fork, rear plunger

Brakes: drum (front and rear)

Weight: approx. 440 lbs

Serge Bueno reflects. "The SS80 is the Rolls-Royce of motorcycles. I bought this gem from a private owner in England, thanks to my brother who has lived in London for twenty years and who seeks out rare pieces for me. The bike was in good condition, but I had to touch up the paintwork, give everything a good polish, and chrome-plate several rusted parts."

In 2019, a French company relaunched this legendary brand. Old soldiers never die. . . .

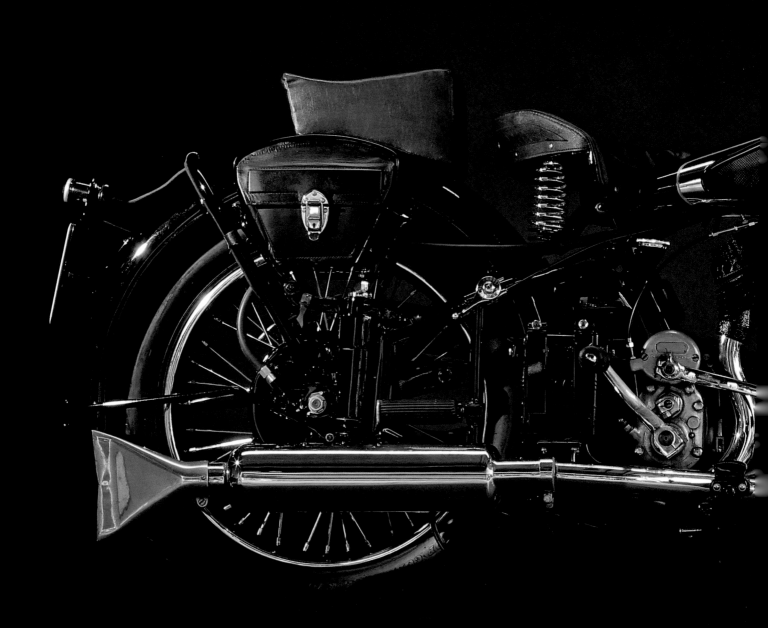

esigned especially for all-terrain racing, the 1938 M18 model shone at the Belgian and French Grand Prix, as well as at the Ulster Grand Prix in Northern Ireland—a race that is nearly as famous as the Isle of Man Tourist Trophy and has a mass start that tends to create some spectacular situations. The M18, which was given a makeover in 1935, had a single-cylinder, air-cooled engine displacing 500 cc (30.5 cu in) and a four-speed gearbox. Its distinction was that the valve elements were protected by an enclosure. It also had a standard lighting system, side-by-side Smiths rev counter and speedometer dials, a longer front fork than the other models, a rigid rear chassis, and an impressively studded tread on the rear tire. This was a powerful and extremely sturdy motorcycle that was later used by the British Army.

"I already owned a Norton 490 cc Model 30, a charismatic machine in motorcycle history, and I was looking for an M18 from the same period," says Serge Bueno. "Not only was I enormously lucky to pick up this little marvel from a private seller in France, but it was in a perfect state. I didn't touch a single thing: not the engine, not the saddlery, not the cabling. A little repaint was all that was needed to restore its edgy look."

IN 1951, ERNESTO GUEVARA—WHO WOULD BECOME BETTER KNOWN AS THE GUERRILLERO "CHE" OF THE CUBAN REVOLUTION—AND HIS FRIEND ALBERTO GRANADO TRAVELED ACROSS SOUTH AMERICA ON A NORTON M18 THEY NICKNAMED *LA PODEROSA* ("THE MIGHTY ONE"). IT WAS AN EPIC JOURNEY DEPICTED IN THE ROAD MOVIE *THE MOTORCYCLE DIARIES*, STARRING GAEL GARCÍA BERNAL AND RODRIGO DE LA SERNA.

The M18 was another classic motorcycle produced by the Norton Motorcycle Company. English flair!

Manufacturer: Norton
Year of production: 1938

<u>ENGINE</u>

Type: single-cylinder, four-stroke, air-cooled
Displacement: 500 cc (30.5 cu in)
Power: 20 hp
Carburetor: Amal
Secondary transmission: chain
Gearbox: four-speed, pedal shifter
Maximum speed: 80 mph

<u>BIKE</u>

Frame: steel, single open cradle
Suspension: parallelogram front fork, rigid rear
Brakes: drum (front and rear)
Weight: approx. 265 lbs

Painted entirely in black, with Firestone fat tires and a very low saddle, the R25 had the sort of aggressive aesthetics that are popular today.

"For me, this 1950 R25 symbolizes the reliability, sturdiness, and power of German motorcycles," explains Serge Bueno. "It is quite something to cruise down the highway at close to 60 mph on a machine weighing 300 lbs. The light restoration work I did on it gave me real joy, because this is the kind of motorcycle you keep for a lifetime."

Manufacturer: BMW
Years of production: 1950–56

ENGINE

Type: single-cylinder, four-stroke, air-cooled, two overhead valves
Displacement: 250 cc (15.25 cu in)
Power: 13 hp
Carburetor: Bing
Secondary transmission: universal joint
Gearbox: four-speed, pedal shifter
Maximum speed: 60 mph

BIKE

Frame: steel, double cradle
Suspension: front telescopic fork, rear plunger
Brakes: drum (front and rear)
Weight: 310 lbs

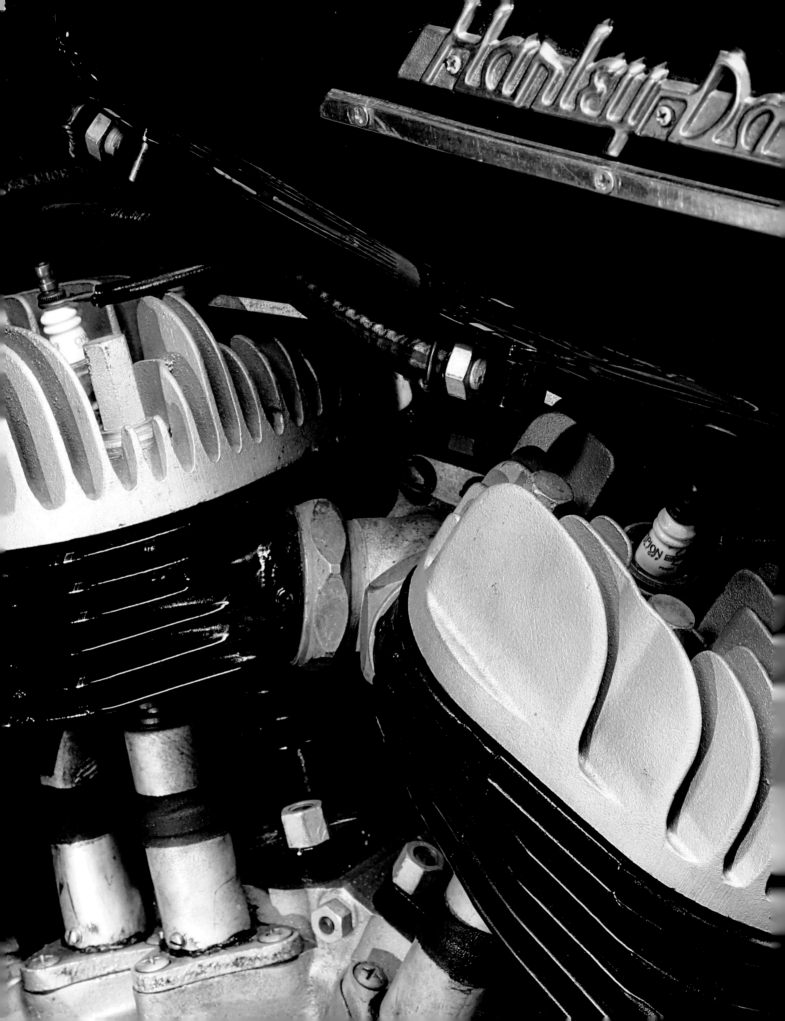

750 cc **WR**

1951

HARLEY-DAVIDSON

COMPANY

Original

BACK TO THE AMERICAN SPEEDWAYS, WHICH WERE NO LONGER MADE OF WOOD, BUT PACKED DIRT THAT OFTEN TURNED TO MUD. THIS IS THE PORTRAIT OF AN INCREDIBLE MACHINE THAT STILL MAKES MOTORCYCLE FANATICS DROOL.

Close-up of the monstrous V-twin of this WR 750, which fought some of the fiercest battles on the dirt tracks.

This legendary racing machine, which was designed especially for dirt tracks, first saw the light of day in 1942. Its one and only mission was to beat the formidable Indian Scout. After years of merciless competition on all the board tracks, the two major brands continued their struggle for supremacy on these muddy circuits. The surface may have changed, but it was still all about opening the throttle to the max—with no front brake—to see who really had the right stuff. And to drive the crowds wild, of course!

With its impressive V-twin made of light alloy—displacing 750 cc (45.75 cu in)—especially developed for racing, a rigid rear frame, and fat tires, the WR was a mean machine, a roaring monster. After the successes of its great rider Joe Petrali in the 1930s, Harley-Davidson had to wait until 1947 to find a new hero: Jimmy Chann, who won the Springfield Mile race—and thus the national championship—three years in a row on his WR 750. Despite the introduction of new models, such as the KR and the XR, the tireless WR fought on until 1973, and fully deserves its status as a cult bike.

In 1951 and 1952, Indian's warrior, Bobby Hill, took the top place on the podium. But it proved to be the manufacturer's swan song, as it shut down production in 1953. This great sporting rivalry, a historic mano a mano that had lasted nearly half a century, was over, leaving behind two epic racing motorcycles: the Indian Scout and the Harley-Davidson WR 750.

Serge Bueno feels a particular affinity for this survivor: "For me this motorcycle symbolizes the incredible battle between Harley and Indian—competition at the highest level between both machines and riders. I must have a lucky star watching over me because I discovered this WR 750, or rather its component pieces, in three different places. I redid everything from top to bottom, respecting its identity down to the last detail. It was a Herculean task. When I photographed it three-quarters on, I felt like it resembled a wild animal ready to leap."

Manufacturer: Harley-Davidson
Year of production: 1951

Type: V-twin, four-stroke, air-cooled
Displacement: 750 cc (45.75 cu in)
Power: 28 hp
Final transmission: chain
Gearbox: three-speed
Maximum speed: 95 mph

BIKE

Frame: steel, single cradle
Suspension: springer front fork, rigid rear
Brakes: rear drum brake
Weight: 350 lbs

THE VINCENT OWNERS CLUB WAS FOUNDED ON THE ISLE OF MAN IN 1948, AFTER A HISTORIC VICTORY BY THE BLACK SHADOW IN THE TOURIST TROPHY. THE 150 MEMBERS OF THE "FAMILY," WITH THEIR OWN LITTLE FACTORY TO MAKE SPARE PARTS, MEET ONCE A YEAR TO CELEBRATE THEIR MECHANICAL IDOL. A PHOTOGRAPH TAKEN IN DOUGLAS IN 1950 IS EVIDENCE OF THE UNCONDITIONAL LOYALTY OF THE RIDERS OF THE MOST BEAUTIFUL MOTORCYCLE IN THE WORLD.

A harmony of black and chrome characterizes this sublime machine that made its mark on its time like no other.

Vincent Motorcycles was the story of three genius enthusiasts who conceived the motorcycle of their dreams. The adventure began with Howard Raymond Davies, who was later joined by Philip Vincent before the arrival of engineer Phil Irving accelerated the process. The trio worked on a brand-new machine: a twin-cylinder displacing 998 cc (60.9 cu in) paired with a four-speed gearbox with foot shifter. This was the 1936 Rapide, which had a cantilever rear suspension.

Twelve years later, the innovations of this Rapide model gave birth to the Black Shadow, a beast of a bike fitted with a four-stroke engine with overhead valves, displacing 998 cc (60.9 cu in). Built entirely by hand, the Black Shadow's engine casing was all in black—supposedly to improve heat rejection from the engine, although the real advantage seems to have been its striking visual impact. It also had a Smiths speedometer. This splendid motorcycle not only won the 1948 Isle of Man Tourist Trophy, but also shattered the American speed record for naturally aspirated motorcycles when the American rider Roland "Rollie" Free achieved a speed of 150.313 mph at the Bonneville Salt Flats in Utah that same year. On his final run, Free even stripped off his racing leathers and lay prone on the bike in order to be as light as possible and to maximize his aerodynamic profile.

"The Vincent Black Shadow is indeed one of the most beautiful and best-performing motorcycles in the world," explains Serge Bueno. "Its renown has only grown with passing years since production ended. At the time, it cost twice as much as the other machines. These days, its rarity has caused its price to soar astronomically. Everybody wants one, from collectors to museums. I was immensely lucky that one of my relatives in rural France owned one. Sure, it was in a deplorable state, but the pleasure I took in completely restoring

Manufacturer: Vincent
Years of production: 1948–54

ENGINE

Type: V-twin, four-stroke, air-cooled
Displacement: 1,000 cc (61 cu in)
Power: 55 hp
Carburetor: 2 x Amal
Transmission: chain (primary and secondary)
Gearbox: four-speed, pedal shifter
Maximum speed: 125 mph

BIKE

Frame: steel box that doubles as an oil tank, with the engine mounted as a stressed member
Suspension: parallelogram front fork, rear cantilever attached to spring boxes beneath the seat and a hydraulic damper
Brakes: 2 x drum (front), 2 x drum (rear)
Weight: 450 lbs

Each hand-built bike is
an example of perfect
craftsmanship.

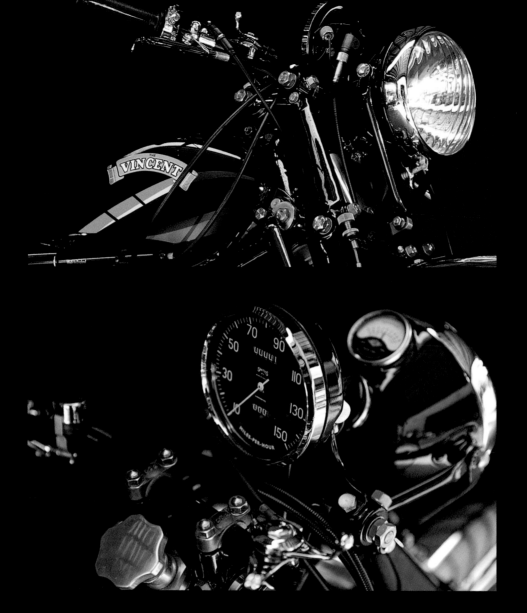

The 150 members of the
Vincent Owners Club can
be rightly proud to own
one of the most beautiful
motorcycles in the world.

200 cc ★ 1955

TRIUMPH
TIGER CUB

IN THE 1950S, THE INROADS MADE BY BRITISH MOTORCYCLES HAD A MAJOR IMPACT ON THE AMERICAN MARKET, PARTICULARLY INDIAN, WHICH CLOSED ITS FACTORIES IN 1953. TRIUMPH ACHIEVED CONSIDERABLE SUCCESS THROUGH IMPROVEMENTS SUCH AS PEDAL-SHIFTED GEARS AND A MANUAL CLUTCH. THE SPORTIER-LOOKING BRITISH BIKES OBLIGED HARLEY-DAVIDSON TO REVIEW ITS ENTIRE PRODUCTION.

You can appreciate the sleek profile and inimitable look of this Tiger Club when it is photographed head-on: one of those beautiful, classy English machines that revolutionized the world of high-end motorcycles.

This Triumph Tiger Cub had a resolutely modern look for the period. It belonged to the breed of motorcycles dubbed "Road and Trail," which was equally comfortable on both surfaces. The Cub, which sold extremely well, is one of those motorcycles that almost never goes out of style. It was fitted with a long-stroke, single-cylinder engine—with the cylinders and cylinder heads made of aluminum—and a four-speed gearbox. The telescopic front fork, the silver enameling, the chrome-plated headlight, the signature red interior of the exhaust, and the small gas tank gave it a sense of class and power so recognizable in British motorcycles.

Manufacturer: Triumph
Years of production: 1954–56

ENGINE

Type: single-cylinder, four-stroke, air-cooled
Displacement: 200 cc (12.2 cu in)
Power: 10 hp
Carburetor: Amal
Transmission: chain (primary and secondary)
Gearbox: four-speed, pedal shifter
Maximum speed: 55 mph

BIKE

Frame: steel, single "keystone" cradle (uses the engine as a stressed member)
Suspension: front telescopic (hydraulic) front fork, rigid rear
Brakes: drum (front and rear)
Weight: 175 lbs

MANX 350 cc
Norton
1955

THIS 350 CC MANX WAS ONE IN A LONG LINE OF CLASSIC MOTORCYCLES THAT MADE NORTON'S NAME AT THE ISLE OF MAN TOURIST TROPHY. PRODUCTION WAS SUSPENDED DURING WORLD WAR II, BUT STARTED UP AGAIN IN 1946 WITH A NEW GENERATION OF EVEN MORE ADVANCED MANX MODELS THAT WOULD PROVE TO BE LETHAL WEAPONS ON THE RACETRACKS.

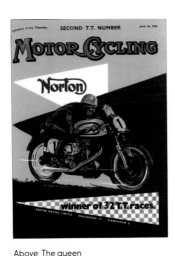

Above: The queen of the Isle of Man TT races on the cover of the British *Motor Cycling* magazine.

Opposite: The Manx's signature exhaust pipe: interior painted red and the outward-facing side cut flat.

erge Bueno spares no praise for this machine, which he calls "a diamond of pure speed in the English crown." According to the sorcerer mechanic of Heroes Motors, "this uncontested queen of the racetracks had a quite specific signature in the form of its unusual exhaust pipe: the interior was painted red, and the outward-facing side was cut flat—instead of rounded— allowing tighter turns to be made without damaging it."

After the addition of the Roadholder telescopic fork, with hydraulic shock absorption, the key modification came in 1949, when the engineer Rex McCandless designed the featherbed frame made of thin, lightweight Reynolds steel tubes. All of these technical improvements enabled the Manx to hold off the more powerful, multicylinder Italian bikes, such as Gilera and Moto Guzzi.

"I must admit that the full restoration of this 1956 Norton Manx remains an unforgettable memory," says Serge Bueno. "I found it in several parts on the Isle of Man—the theater of its past exploits. It took me nearly a month of work to restore its luster and class. It was an extremely sophisticated machine with a four-stroke, single-cylinder engine displacing 350 cc (21.35 cu in). The incredibly complicated double overhead camshaft cost me many an all-nighter. The restoration of the gas tank—also a very particular design—was no picnic, either. But I am supremely proud to have resuscitated this classic bike."

Type: single-cylinder, four-stroke, air-cooled

Displacement: 350 cc (21.35 cu in)

Power: 38 hp

Carburetor: Amal GP

Transmission: chain (primary and secondary)

Gearbox: four-speed, pedal shifter

Maximum speed: 120 mph

BIKE

Frame: steel, double cradle

Suspension: telescopic front fork, plunger rear

Brakes: 2 x drum (front), single drum (rear)

Weight: 315 lbs

ISLE OF MAN TOURIST TROPHY

ONE TRACK ONLY

Located in the Irish Sea between Great Britain and Ireland, this Celtic land has been the scene of the most dangerous motorcycle road race in the world since 1907. Initially, the race covered a fifteen-mile course starting and finishing in the village of St. John's. In 1911, the race switched to the longer Snaefell Mountain Course of 37.73 miles, comprising 264 turns, where riders made six laps, for a total of more than 226 miles flat out. The best riders in the world gathered here each year in the first week of June to pit themselves against one another in this crazy race, which was part of the world championships. These riders on their speed machines took insane risks as they zipped through villages at full throttle, even becoming airborne as they hit bumps, and crashing out on the tightest corners. In 1972, the death of the rider Gilberto Parlotti led to a boycott of the event by the top riders and the Tourist Trophy was removed from the calendar of the World Motorcycle Championship. Since 1911 there has been a tragic record of over 250 rider deaths during the course of this hellish race.

These days, the TT is for amateur motorcyclists only, but both amateurs and professionals can compete in the Manx Grand Prix, another speed race on the Isle of Man that began in 1923.

╳ INDEX ╳

Serge Bueno would like to thank Bobby Haas, Matthew Katz, Peter Lenkov, Geraldo Targino, Éric Levi, Patrick Guetta, Éric Bueno, Bruno Cherqui, René Hagege, Alex Nastat, Xavier Parent, Gilles Lhote, Philippe Marchand. And very special thanks to Muriel and to my children, Anthony, Carla, Matt and Michael.

PICTURE CREDITS